Index on Censorship

Free Word Centre, 60 Farringdon Road, London, ECIR 3GA

Chief Executive John Kampfner **Deputy Chief Executive** Rohan Jayasekera **Editor** Jo Glanville **Finance Manager** David Sewell **Head of Events** Sara Rhodes **Online Editor** Emily Butselaar **News Editor** Padraig Reidy **Assistant Editor** Natasha Schmidt **Head of Advocacy** Michael Harris **Head of Development** Lizzie Rusbridger **Head of Communications** Pam Cowburn **Programme Manager, Arts** Julia Farrington **Events Assistant** Eve Jackson **Editorial Assistants** Marta Cooper, Sara Yasin **Research Assistant** Carlette Jannink **Interns** Olga Birukova, Michael Johnson, Alice-May Purkiss **US Editor** Emily Badger **US Head of Development** Bridget Gallagher

Graphic designer Sam Hails
Cover design Brett Biedscheid
Printed by Page Bros., Norwich, UK

Volume 40 No 4 2011

If you are interested in republishing any article featured in this issue, please contact us at permissions@indexoncensorship.org

Supported by
ARTS COUNCIL ENGLAND

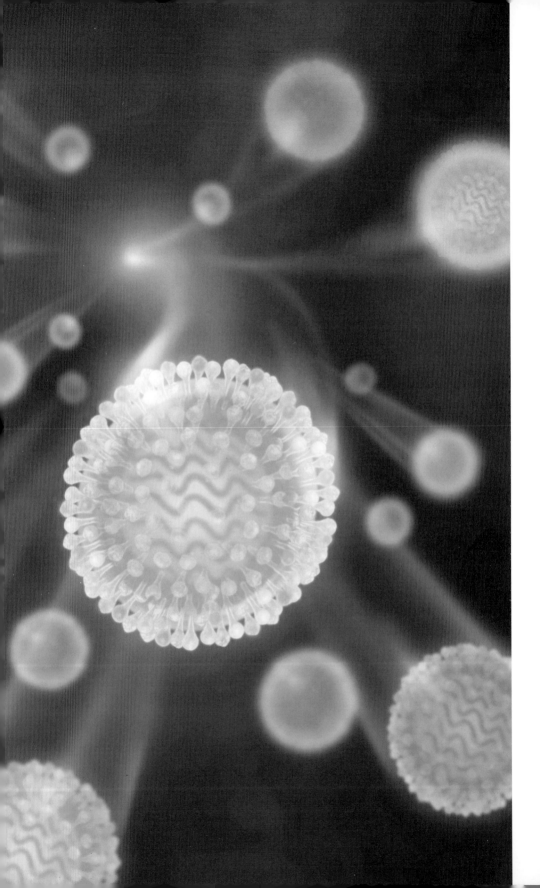

DATA CONTROL

Jo Glanville

When Index on Censorship launched its libel reform campaign with English PEN two years ago, it was the scientists facing legal action who particularly caught the attention of the press and public. Suddenly libel was not just a matter of stifling press freedom, it could be a case of life or death: with evidence that scientists were being stopped from speaking out, censorship has become an issue of public health and safety. Tracey Brown, whose organisation Sense About Science has been central to the continuing campaign for reform, illustrates just how damaging litigation can be for scientists and how frequently it has become a tool to intimidate and silence criticism [pp. 40–47]: 'The expansion of science communication has been met by efforts to close down inconvenient evidence – through commercial pressure, intimidation, vandalism of research, sackings and threats of court proceedings.' The scientist Richard Dawkins and the journal *Nature* are among the most recent defendants to face libel actions.

Within the science community, some of the most celebrated scientists also consider Freedom of Information (FOI) requests to be part of the armoury of current intimidation tactics. Nobel laureate and president of the Royal Society Sir Paul Nurse said earlier this year that FOI was being used to harass scientists and has called for new guidelines. Yet as the leading science writer Fred Pearce observes in his article for *Index*, it's an argument that is becoming increasingly hard to maintain, particularly since the information commissioner ruled that the Climate Research Unit (CRU) at the University of East Anglia should release its data [pp. 113–119]. It was the furore over 'climategate' two years ago, when the CRU's emails were hacked, that first revealed the level of resistance of some scientists to sharing information.

As Pearce points out, 'the whole point of research is that it should be open to maximum scrutiny' – and the irony is that scientists, more than anyone, have been at the forefront of the information revolution that has made data sharing possible on a scale never seen before.

REUTERS/Arko Datta

TRUSTLAW

EMPOWERING PEOPLE THROUGH INFORMATION

Looking for high-impact pro bono opportunities in your country or elsewhere?
Or free legal assistance?

Interested in the latest on women's rights and corruption worldwide?

TrustLaw is a free global service designed to make it simpler for lawyers to engage in pro bono work and easier for NGOs and social entrepreneurs to access free legal assistance.

TrustLaw is also a global hub of news and information on good governance, anti-corruption and women's rights from our correspondents and content partners. The site includes articles, blogs, case studies, multimedia and country profiles.

trust.org/trustlaw

© 2011 Thomson Reuters L-358831/5-10

Thomson Reuters Foundation is the charitable arm of Thomson Reuters and operator of TrustLaw and TrustLaw Connect.

THOMSON REUTERS FOUNDATION

While some scientists claim that FOI requests may jeopardise their research, lack of transparency within the healthcare industry remains a major concern. The *BMJ*'s Deborah Cohen has done remarkable work for her own publication as well as Panorama and Channel 4 to investigate the secrecy within the pharmaceutical and medical devices industry. She brings her investigations together for the first time in her piece for *Index*, revealing the consequences of what can happen when critical evidence is unavailable to the medical profession [pp. 59–72].

In the US, Heather Weaver reveals the tactics used by the creationist lobby to push their influence – a battle that has continued since the famous Scopes trial of 1925. Despite the defeat of creationists since then to win in court, they have developed sophisticated means of spreading their message and there is worrying evidence of their influence on the American public – according to a study published by *Science* in January, 60 per cent of public school biology teachers 'legitimise creationist arguments'.

Also in this issue, as the Leveson inquiry into the ethics of the media continues in the UK, Julian Petley talks to the distinguished lawyer Sir Louis Blom-Cooper about regulating the press. Blom-Cooper was appointed head of the Press Council at the end of the 80s, one of the last times there was a national crisis about the ethics of the press – his insights into the current climate are worth considering. We're also delighted to publish celebrated Dutch-Moroccan author Abdelkader Benali's views on the origins of the Arab spring, alongside fiction and essays from North Africa and Iran. You can follow Index on Censorship as always on our website for the latest stories on censorship around the world www.indexoncensorship.org ❐

©Jo Glanville
40(4): 1/5
DOI: 10.1177/0306422011428856
www.indexoncensorship.org

CONTENTS

DISPATCHES

DARK MATTER

FIRST PERSON

INDEX INDEX

*Darwin v Intelligent Design: Parents in Dover, Pennsylvania, sued the school board
for trying to introduce creationism to the school curriculum, December 2005
Credit: Sipa Press/Rex Features*

DISPATCHES

The UK media under scrutiny:
haven't we been here before?

Abdelkader Benali on the Arab spring:
seeds of the revolutions

LESSONS FOR LEVESON

As British journalists face the most significant public inquiry in a generation, **Julian Petley** talks to former Press Council chief **Louis Blom-Cooper**

The Leveson inquiry, whose remit includes examining 'the culture, practices, and ethics of the press', as well as making recommendations for a 'new more effective policy and regulatory regime which supports the integrity and freedom of the press', represents a twice-in-a-lifetime opportunity to reform the behaviour of the press and the manner in which it is regulated. Why twice? Because we've actually been here before.

During the 80s, intrusive and generally excessive behaviour by the popular press led to a growing number of calls in Parliament for newspapers to be regulated more effectively. In 1981, Frank Allaun introduced what was to be the first of a series of private members' Bills calling for a statutory right of reply for members of the public against whom allegations had been made in the media as a whole; Austin Mitchell introduced a similar Bill in 1984, and in 1987 Ann Clwyd brought forward her Unfair Reporting and Right of Reply Bill. These were all Labour MPs, but in 1987 the Tory MP William Cash presented his Right of Privacy Bill, and the following year another Tory, John Browne, introduced a Protection of Privacy Bill, closely followed by Labour MP Tony Worthington's Right of Reply Bill.

In 1980, the Campaign for Press and Broadcasting Freedom set up an independent inquiry into the Press Council, chaired by Geoffrey Robertson QC. This produced the highly critical report *People Against the Press*, which called for the Council to be given considerably sharper teeth and for the creation of a statutory press ombudsman, as well as for a Freedom of Information Act and the relaxation of laws which hindered investigative reporting. (In the present context, this is a work which urgently needs revisiting.) In February 1987, Lord Longford initiated a debate on press standards in the Lords, and in July of the same year Labour forced a debate in the Commons on Murdoch's acquisition of the *Today* newspaper.

By the late 1980s, loud demands for press reform were therefore very firmly on the political and social agenda. This led to the appointment in 1988 of the eminent QC Sir Louis Blom-Cooper as the new head of the Press Council, with the aim of making it a more respected, authoritative and effective self-regulatory body. Like Geoffrey Robertson, Blom-Cooper was concerned both to protect, and indeed to enlarge, the freedom to practise serious journalism which was clearly in the public interest, but also to provide forms of redress for those who had been the victims of mere muckraking and scandalmongering.

The problem was, however, that the popular press cared little for the former kind of journalism but was determined to protect the latter at all costs. Thus Blom-Cooper's reforms not only found little support amongst owners and editors (and by no means only at the popular end of the market), but he himself became the target of press mischief-making, both in the newspapers themselves and, more damagingly still, behind the scenes in Westminster and Whitehall. Thus the Council was described in the newspapers it was supposed to be regulating as consisting of 'pompous laymen and self-important journalists', as straying 'too far into the jungles of taste and discretion', as a 'bunch of loonies' (the *Sun*, inevitably) and as issuing 'hectoring encyclicals'.

Seemingly showing little faith in Blom-Cooper's reforms, in 1989 the government responded to the growing clamour over press misbehaviour by establishing a committee of inquiry under Sir David Calcutt QC, whose remit was to 'consider what measures (whether legislative or otherwise) are needed to give further protection to individual privacy from the activities of the press and improve recourse against the press for the individual citizen'. The writing was clearly on the wall for the Council, and indeed Calcutt was to recommend its abolition and its replacement by the Press Complaints Commission, a body with, to the delight of the press, an even narrower remit than its predecessor, being an organisation which was concerned solely with receiving, mediating and adjudicating on complaints.

The press attitude to Louis Blom-Cooper's reforms demonstrated all too clearly that the newspaper owners and editors simply would not countenance any self-regulatory measure of which they themselves did not approve. Furthermore, they used their considerable political influence to help into existence a neutered body with which they would feel considerably more at ease. And as absolutely nothing has changed, at least for the better, since the death of the Press Council and the birth of the PCC, this immediately raises a crucial question: even if Leveson does come up with proposals for effective press reform, would the government be prepared to enact them in the teeth of massive, daily press hostility? Past experience suggests that it would not. Even now the knives are out for Leveson in papers such as the *Daily Mail*, and it's likely that the government is being relentlessly lobbied by the press barons behind Leveson's back. Indeed, given that one of the other matters which Leveson is investigating is 'the relationship between national newspapers and politicians', he already has a ready-made case study right under his nose.

Julian Petley: What opportunities for press reform do you think are presented by the Leveson Inquiry?

Louis Blom-Cooper: In my view, Leveson presents us with a golden opportunity to do something on the grand scale. All the focus on the press has been, for historical reasons, on complaints, but handling complaints is a disciplinary function, it's not about monitoring or supervising. What the public needs is to know what its press is doing on its behalf, and also what it is *not* doing – for example, the reporting of the activities of government prior to the war in Iraq, about which we were left almost totally in the dark because newspapers were not reporting them.

Julian Petley: There has been a great deal of discussion about whether any new arrangements should be independent, self-regulatory or statutory. What's your view?

Louis Blom-Cooper: I go absolutely spare when people say that whatever intervention there is it must be non-statutory. This is a total nonsense. It depends entirely on what the statute seeks to achieve and what it contains. I also think we need to get rid of the word 'regulation'; what we actually need is an

DAILY EXPRESS

THE VOICE OF BRITAIN

pper squad police escort man to court...

handcuffed to a detective and with his head covered by a blanket, passes through the police cordon. Picture by TOM SMITH

ORDEAL OF WIFE

A WIFE waiting in court yesterday

By Peggie Robinson

THE NEW STANDARD

Incorporating the Evening News

Monday, January 5, 1981. Price 17p

Lorry driver to appear in court too

RIPPER: MA WAS QUIZZED 4 TIMES

A PORTRAIT picture of the prepared in one of the women

Daily Mail

MONDAY, JANUARY 5, 1981   12p

CHARITY AND THE HIGH LIFE

uestion driver found in car with woman

IPPER—A AN RRESTED

Jubilee gathering last night: Oldfield, Gregory, Hobson

ere last night an in connection shire Ripper have claimed 13 in five years.

By AUBERT TUROSA

court today on what a very serious charge: Gregory, Yorkshire and the officers arrested in the

---

DAILY Mirror

Monday, January 5, 1981   12p

Suspect i held by vice patro

RIPPER HUN MAN IN COURT

A MAN held for questioning by hunting the Yorkshire Ripper is appear in court today.

THE Sun

Monday, January 5, 1981   12p   TODAY'S 7p PAGES 12 and 13

EXCLUSIVE TODAY!

5 SUPER FORDS TO BE WON
PAGE 24

METRO MEN VOTE TO GO BACK
See Page 2

WILD WEST ONE

Behind the closed doors of the rich and the famous—Pages 15-18

EXCLUSIVE TO GET A THONE A MATCHBOX
Page 14

AND COMING YOUR WAY THIS WEEK ... See Pages 2, 3, 7, 9, 11, 13.

DAILY rror

12p

THE MAN CUSED

RIPPER: MAN FACES COURT TODAY

A MARRIED man was being questioned last night by detectives hunting the Yorkshire Ripper who has killed 13 women.

'Red light' arre

independent body which carries out monitoring – independent monitoring of the press. The word 'regulation' implies, I think, to some people, some form of executive power, and what I would propose does not contain executive power.

Any form of public intervention to create such a body would require legislation in the first instance. But one absolutely does not want the supervision to be carried out by government itself, rather the government should establish an independent, standing body by means of statute, namely a Commission. The statute establishing the Commission would also set up an Appointments Commission which would consist of, for example, the chairmen of the British Library, the British Museum, the Association of Vice-Chancellors and Principals of Universities, the Lord Chief Justice of England, the Lord President of the Court of Sessions; they wouldn't be specifically named people, but the people who held these offices at the time of selection. One would thus put between the institution of government and the public itself a wholly independent body, independently selected.

Julian Petley: What powers would this body have?

Louis Blom-Cooper: This brings us back to the nature of the body itself. I would have a standing Royal Commission composed of people who were entirely independent of publishing in any form and appointed in the fashion which I've just mentioned. And it should certainly include members of the public; half of the people appointed to the Press Council were members of the public, and every year we used to receive more than 1,000 applications. This certainly wasn't replicated in the PCC. As I've said, this body should be conceived on the grand scale. For example, it should be involved in the question of the education and training of journalists, and in ensuring that there is plurality of press ownership, so that in the case of mergers they can examine whether or not they should take place. In all of these matters it should be undertaking investigations, not exercising executive power. What I do think vitally important would be the Commission's ability to conduct public inquiries, and the statute would have to give it all the necessary procedural powers to conduct such inquiries, in particular the power to subpoena witnesses. These are what the Press Council sadly, and damagingly, lacked when it carried out its inquiries into press behaviour in the Peter Sutcliffe case and the 1990 Strangeways Prison riot. These would be statutory powers, but they would be procedural, they wouldn't deal with the substance.

Julian Petley: How would the Commission be funded?

Louis Blom-Cooper: The Commission would have to be funded by Parliament, to whom it would be answerable, and they would have to go to Parliament every year with their budget, just as the Supreme Court has to do, to ask for money to support their activities. So it would have to be funded out of the public purse and not, for example, by a levy on the newspapers: one doesn't want the press to have any interest, as it were, in the activities of this body. My parallel here, structurally and constitutionally, would be the Standing Royal Commission on the Environment, which is constantly looking at what's happening to the environment, or PhonepayPlus [formerly known as ICSTIS], the regulatory body for all premium rate phone-paid services in the United Kingdom.

Julian Petley: Would the Commission deal with complaints against individual newspapers?

Louis Blom-Cooper: No doubt one of the Commission's functions might involve receiving and adjudicating on complaints, but I don't think that complaints are what really matters here. And, incidentally, insofar as complaints do matter, in my view the first clause of the PCC Code, which has to do with accuracy, is far more important than the one pertaining to privacy. The real problem is the daily lying, cheating and distorting in the press, all of which fall under the first clause of the Code.

Julian Petley: Indeed. Let's just remind ourselves of what this actually says: (i) The press must take care not to publish inaccurate, misleading or distorted information, including pictures. (ii) A significant inaccuracy, misleading statement or distortion once recognised must be corrected, promptly and with due prominence, and – where appropriate – an apology published. In cases involving the Commission, prominence should be agreed with the PCC in advance. (iii) The press, whilst free to be partisan, must distinguish clearly between comment, conjecture and fact. Now, this is trampled on daily and routinely treated with absolute contempt, particularly by the popular press. You have only to open any popular paper with the code beside you to realise the yawning chasm between the rule and the reality. Thus it's entirely unsurprising that the PCC's own statistics reveal that, in 2009, 87.2 per cent of the complaints which it received concerned accuracy and opportunity to reply, and only 23.7 per cent were about privacy.

Louis Blom-Cooper: Indeed, but I'm not sure that I'd necessarily get rid of the PCC under the arrangements which I've just outlined – if the industry itself

The last edition of News International's tabloid News of the World, Sunday, 10 July 2011
Credit: Michael Kemp/Alamy

wishes to deal with complaints against its members, why the hell shouldn't it? It seems to me a perfectly sensible exercise on the part of any employer to want to know what is in fact happening amongst his own employees. On the other hand, it does need to be stressed that self-regulation in the newspaper industry has proved to be self-serving; it aims to protect the newspaper industry from anything that would impose responsible conduct on proprietors, editors and journalists by an independent agency. It has palpably not served the public interest. And the PCC Code is constructed entirely within the newspaper industry for the benefit of its practitioners, rather than as a standard bearer of ethical behaviour for the public.

But the really important point about the body which I'm advocating is that the statutory power which it would have would be non-executive, that is to say that it would have no direct control over journalists or editors – it would act by precept. Its main function would be monitoring – looking at the press day in and day out and telling the public what it is and, equally importantly, isn't, doing. It could organise conferences with practitioners in journalism. It would keep under review all the laws affecting the press. It would make representation to the Competition Commission in cases involving takeovers. It should promote centres for the advanced study of and research in journalism. In all these things the Commission would aim to assist the newspaper industry in defining a set of workable standards, and to act as a forum for public debate on the freedom of the press.

It really is extremely important to understand, as I said in my 2007 lecture in honour of Professor Harry Street ['regulation of the media is entirely compatible with, indeed required by, society's commitment to the values of freedom of speech. There is a need for a new watchdog which barks authoritatively, and, where appropriate, in stentorian terms, but does not bite, except indirectly and influentially'].

Julian Petley: I would agree entirely, but unfortunately the press has done its absolute utmost to equate regulation with censorship.

Louis Blom-Cooper: Yes it has, but what I'm talking about has nothing to do with controlling the press, because I regard all press freedom as simply a manifestation of our individual freedom; that is to say, we give to the press the duty to practise collectively and on our behalf the freedom of expression which we all possess under Article 10 of the European Convention on Human Rights. Freedom of speech belongs to all of us, it belongs equally to those who work in the media and to those who don't. It's particularly important to understand that such a conception of freedom of expression rules out the licensing of journalists. As Harry Street himself argued in *Freedom, the Individual and the Law*, journalism is 'the exercise by occupation of the right to free expression available to every citizen. That right, being available to all, cannot in principle be withdrawn from a few by any system of licensing or professional registration'. No one can be prevented from exercising free speech other than by a law which applies to everybody. But, of course, there's nothing *necessarily* wrong in restricting and confining freedom of expression by rules of law which do apply to everyone. If freedom of the press means no more than our collective rights performed on our behalf by those daily engaged in newsgathering, then we (the public), in the form of democratic government, should determine how far we should restrict our collective rights, and how the press is to be monitored and supervised. And it is certainly the case that current concerns about the standards of journalism suffice to demand both public debate and governmental action.

Julian Petley: Again, I would agree, but unfortunately the way in which press owners and their appointed editors understand press freedom in this country has precious little to do with Article 10. What they appear to mean by press freedom is the freedom to do just what the hell they like with the newspapers which they own and run. What we have here is in fact simply a smokescreen, the assertion of a property right in the guise of a free speech right, and an extremely arrogant claim that newspapers should be immune from regulations which apply to everyone else.

Louis Blom-Cooper: But such a position is wholly untenable. Tell me where, constitutionally, do they get that idea from? Maybe things have developed in this fashion, but tell me what is the legal basis for the present state of affairs? The only legal basis for freedom of the press is Article 10.

Julian Petley: Of course, but the kind of people to whom I'm referring don't give a damn about Article 10 – all they're concerned with is the threat posed by Article 8 to their commercial lifeblood of kiss 'n' tell stories. Indeed, they want the government to rip up the Human Rights Act (HRA) and to withdraw from the European Convention on Human Rights, and their papers are filled day in and day out with the most poisonous and ill-informed stories peddling this particular line. The fact that British newspapers clearly hate the whole notion of human rights tells you everything you need to know about the fundamentally populist, illiberal and indeed anti-democratic nature of much of the British press.

Louis Blom-Cooper: Maybe, but the press's argument is hopeless, because they're caught by the Human Rights Act whether they like it or not. And the whole campaign against both the Act and the Convention is just historically illiterate and utter nonsense. One of the things which I found most disappointing about Ed Miliband's speech at this year's Labour conference was that there was absolutely no acknowledgement of probably the best thing that Labour did when it was in office, namely to introduce the Human Rights Act. There's Nick Clegg nailing his flag to the mast of the HRA, and delightfully so, but how much better it would have been if Miliband had said that 'we are the architects of the HRA and we have no intention ever of seeing it destroyed'.

Julian Petley: Which they'll never say, because they wake up every morning terrified of what has been written about them in the right-wing press. What Leveson really needs to investigate is how we've arrived at a situation in

Actor Hugh Grant speaks about phone hacking for the 'Hacked Off' campaign, Conservative Party conference, Manchester, UK, 4 October 2011
Credit: Stefan/Rousseau/PA Wire

which, thanks to politicians' pusillanimity in the face of newspaper bullying, the likes of Paul Dacre, who is accountable only to his readers, effectively dictate government policy on a wide range of social issues. However, turning back to Leveson, do you think that the Calcutt Inquiry, the death of the Press Council and the subsequent creation of the Press Complaints Commission hold any lessons for the present moment?

Louis Blom-Cooper: The Calcutt Committee came to the conclusion that a body like the Press Council which, under my chairmanship, was promoting the freedom of the press was incompatible with a complaints body. And that was the reason for getting rid of it – the newspaper industry did not like the way that I was wanting to take the Council, to make it a public body which, whilst dealing with complaints, was very much there for the public. In other words, its primary function was not to protect the industry but to give the public something which they could recognise and accept with confidence as being on their side. So it was in the industry's interest that the PCC was established, and from my very first day at the Council prominent people in the newspaper industry set about getting rid of me. And when Calcutt was set up, the industry saw this as the perfect opportunity to further their interests in the abolition of the Press Council. ❑

Louis Blom-Cooper's lecture 'Press Freedom: Constitutional Right or Cultural Assumption?', the 22nd Street Lecture, given at the University of Manchester, 23 November 2007, is reproduced in Public Law *(2008), pp. 260–76*

©Julian Petley
40(4): 14/24
DOI: 10.1177/0306422011428552
www.indexoncensorship.org

Julian Petley is head of research journalism at Brunel University. He is the author of *Censorship* (Oneworld) and a member of Index's advisory board

CENTRE FOR INVESTIGATIVE JOURNALISM

FILM cij
WEEK
25-29 JANUARY 2012
CITY UNIVERSITY LONDON
TICKETS: £5, WEEKLY PASS AVAILABLE

For a chance to see some of the best investigative work, meet the filmmakers and come to our networking party, please sign up to our newsletter to receive a film line up shortly.

More details on: www.tcij.org/filmweek2012

SPEED DATING HISTORY

Novelist and journalist **Abdelkader Benali** reflects on the origins of a watershed that brought revolution to the Arab world

I visited Tunis in the mid-noughties, responding to an invitation from the Dutch embassy to engage with Tunisian authors and their students. We gathered at a hotel in Habib Bourguiba Avenue, in the centre of the city. The venue was imposing, and so were the authors' positions – a bit too imposing in fact for such a small country as Tunisia. The title of the seminar, 'The role of the writer in contemporary society', sounded even more pompous in French, the language of discourse. It was an unforgettable trip, but for the wrong reasons. There did not seem much to discuss, except the obligatory *l'art pour l'art*, art for art's sake, positions. Nobody really seemed to distinguish which society we had to address, let alone define the adjective 'contemporary'.

Most of the Tunisian writers spoke from their papers, something prepared between a heavy dinner and a nightmare. Their voices sounded shallow, timid, eloquently void of any meaning and brutally grey – they talked like bureaucrats of the police state, not like writers, betraying all they should stand for. But I felt that I could not attack them, taking into consideration that their colleagues in Morocco, Algeria and Iraq were doing the same thing; the ones who spoke up and broke the discourse of taboo and censorship would

*A protester waves the Egyptian flag hours before President Mubarak steps down
from office, Tahrir Square, Cairo, Egypt, 11 February 2011*
Credit: James May/Alamy

be picked up by the secret service for a deflowerment of the mind. They would be thrown in jail, their families' lives would be turned into hell and not a single NGO or western government would have the power to win them amnesty. The American war on terror was broadened by the Arab regimes into a shameless war on everything that went against the status quo.

Wandering through a semi-totalitarian state has its moments of wonder and moments of infantilism. Managing a dictatorship means preserving an absurdist system that turns the citizen, and visitor, into an absurdist personalty. When you train people not to see the problem, it's not the problem that disappears, but the ability to see.

There was one female writer who just whispered her position. And some of the writers would clasp their hands on the table in a futile attempt to bring rhythm to their ramshackle clichés. Hundreds of young female students looked on in silence without moving a finger or raising an eyebrow. The writers of the Union des Ecrivains whom I met just thanked me for coming without detailing what I was to be thanked for. My family name is Benali, the same name as the Tunisian dictator, and it would take people by surprise.

After my speech and talk with literature students (99 per cent women, no headscarves to be seen) I was approached by state television, Channel 7, for a short interview. The interviewer rattled off questions in Arabic and I felt that I had to explain to her that my Arabic wasn't up to doing an interview. She did not look amused, as if I had just told her that Tunisia was a misspelling of amnesia. 'But we could speak French,' I suggested. No reply and an awkward silence.

'I am sorry,' she said after some helpless pondering, 'but we can only interview somebody whose surname is Benali in Arabic.' It didn't help when I wanted to talk about the effects of the channel Al Jazeera on the region at dinner with the writers. They fell still, looking sullen and shocked and downright scared; one of them raised his finger to the ceiling, his gesture meaning this was not the place to talk about these things. 'Let's talk in a café,' he said afterwards and disappeared, never to be seen again, café or no café. These were troubling events: I was invited by the Dutch embassy but hardly found an environment for a free exchange of ideas and opinions.

The Arab revolts are an undeniable fact: they happened. It was 100 per cent manmade – non-violent and almost pedestrian in its demands. Men, women and children stood side by side in a successful attempt to silence the machine guns of the system. People sacrificed their lives to make the

Caricature of Colonel Gaddafi, Tripoli, Libya, 27 August 2011
Credit: Teun Voeten/Panos

unimaginable imaginable, the unthinkable real. The consequences of what happened in several North African and Middle Eastern countries will be felt for years to come. Maybe when another generation is ready to sum up the hope and pitfalls of our time, they will single out this year for two facts only: the death of Steve Jobs and the people of Tahrir Square, both capable of stirring the emotions and imagination of people, both birthgivers to a new era. The uprisings dealt a blow to conspiracy theories because this time the news didn't come from outside to infiltrate people's minds, it came from inside, homemade and exported to the rest of the world.

It's the start of a new epoch in citizen journalism: using their mobiles, Al Jazeera Arabic and English, their Skype and their YouTube, protesters sent messages of anguish, anxiety, despair, heroism and single-mindedness to the world. It's the beginning and it's the continuing of the democratic experiment in the Arab world. It's the women's revolution, highly educated, fluent in languages, fluent in giving language to anger. They were more fearless in the crowd than anybody else. They managed to engage a new audience as witnesses to liberation, not seen since the war in Nicaragua or the struggle against apartheid in South Africa.

The Arab revolts are a conspiracy of action. No place for silence, which is deeply significant: growing up in the cultural environment of an Arab police state means living with silence, learning a strange language of messages in code in which everything is concealed, everything is told. Speaking spontaneously without holding back is almost seen as an act of blasphemy. For this reason, so many young men turned in their flocks to the protecting walls of the mosques where everything was encrypted in religious language. Before you learn anything, you learn that silence is the start and end of every conversation. Things not said cannot be used against you. Walls have ears, streets have ears, shops have ears, the newspaper has no mouth.

From Rabat to Baghdad, the vow of silence has been broken. Until recently the square was the place where one had to be silent, it was an open place but devoid of action and agitation. Before the mass demonstrations of the 14 March generation in 2005 in Lebanon, with more than 100,000 people filling the Square of Martyrs in downtown Beirut, the Arab square seemed nothing more than a place where children, women and the old would gather. The square became the defining place of Arab youth, coming from all corners of society, flooding the space with a myriad of meaning and content. The square was a place where censorship fails; it's too crowded. This cannot be taken away: the people of Tunis and Tahrir and Aden liberated the square with their voices.

A young population, empowered by social media and supported by a plethora of mass media, managed to address the needs and rights of all the people in a grassroots idiom – that's the Arab spring in a nutshell. And we, in the West, stand amazed at the speed dating with history. Not surprisingly, their call for freedom and human dignity managed to engage the West rather than their own governments, which were cautious and behaved roughly towards the people of the Arab world. Citizens in the West associated what they saw with the historic images of East Germans tearing down the wall, while their governments responded erratically: though not insensitive to the lethargy of the Arab world, they were initially willing to help the Arab puppet masters sustain the status quo.

The brutal bargain is no more, where Arab rulers agreed to protect the southern borders of Europe in exchange for their western counterparts' blindness towards human rights violations. Over the past ten years, the Arab world has been viewed through the windows of terrorism, fundamentalism and stagnation. New windows have been added, called freedom, conflict and liberty. And there was something spontaneous and creative in this peaceful uprising. 'President Mubarak, come back, we were joking,' was the quip after his abdication. As the tension grew in Tahrir Square the density of jokes increased with it.

The influence of Al Jazeera as a non-political partisan operator was deeply instrumental in making the revolutions a success. Even before the attacks of 9/11 many young people, urban and non-urban, secular and non-secular, saw in Al Jazeera a new form of guerilla journalism that represented their fight against the lies and taboos of the regimes. Al Jazeera won new respect with the man in the street – the one who waits for his bus for hours and hours, waits for a company to give him 15 minutes to beg for a job and waits in the coffee house for something to turn up. He was looking for a media outlet that would scandalise the regimes, using language and images to commemorate the sufferings of anonymous people on a daily basis: in the Arab world the idea was widespread that the loss of an Arab's life didn't count anymore, that he had no name, no identity. The Arab victim was not reflected in the mirror of the world. Al Jazeera understood this by personalising the anonymous victim – 24 hours a day, seven days a week. Repetition was its success.

But something still seemed lacking, a story of triumph, a defining story of the dead coming back to haunt the living, to haunt the powerful. It was Sidi Bouzid who became the Frankenstein of Tunisia, of the Arab world, whose death sparked the first protests. Al Jazeera was quick to bring social media into play, using the voice of the man in the street and images captured on mobile phones to create the all-encompassing narrative of millions of Frankensteins haunting the regimes.

The generation of Tunis, Cairo, Benghazi and Damascus speaks truth to power. The protesters, as a Syrian freedom fighter commented, were not afraid, because they understood what they were fighting for. Simply to understand what you are willing to give up your life for is devoutly to be wished. Simply having this focus, a non-material focus, but one that encompasses the need to give life to what was considered death: freedom, dignity and the coming together of these two values. Dignity, *karam* in Arabic, is deeply felt in the body, as a necessary organ that preserves some idea of humanness; without it, the ability to truly communicate is lost. And dignity became the opposite of corrupt, something that cannot be contaminated by corruption.

What binds the uprisings, or awakenings, is a collective revolt against the organised crimes of the Arab regimes that was long in the making. The cancer in the marrow is called corruption. What democracy is for Europe, corruption is for the Arab world. There is too much of it. Before you learn anything about the sociological framework of your society, of your kinship, of your connection to the world, everybody makes you understand that the X-ray of it will reveal corruption. The winners are corrupted, the losers are corrupted. The child who grows up aware of his immense talents, finds out sooner or later that the only thing that stands between him and the fulfilment of his family's promise is corruption. It's an undefined line, a rhizome that gnaws and bends through all layers of Arab society, public space, media. The presence of corruption.

Silence is the start and end of every conversation

The uprisings did not come out of the blue; historical movements that shake the ground never occur accidentally. Between 2006 and 2011 Egypt – the country that holds the biggest hope for the region – saw a chain of worker protests. Strikes every week in the little villages at the shores of the Nile. There was economic growth in Egypt, which even managed to keep its head above the waters of the economic 2008 meltdown, but the same could not be said of the poor and the young middle class.

Long before the intellectual anguish the psychological anguish had set in and given hordes of people reason to flee. Over the past 20 years (long years!), North African countries saw the flight of young males towards Europe, a different kind of revolt. From the shores of Morocco, Algeria, Tunisia, Libya and Egypt, thousands of young men left their country in pursuit of an immigrant happiness. With them, many young artists, writers, musicians and thinkers left for fear of persecution, fake trials and discrimination. They found refuge and hope in the welcoming arms of the western intelligentsia who considered them the new exile elite, ready to fill the space left by the former writers of Eastern Europe after the fall of the wall. Though there were misunderstandings, the West was celebrating the end of history, and trying to find a new antidote to the postmodernist hangover. The economy would not be the garden of Eden.

Arab intellectuals were seen as victims but not the prime victim; the real victims were the western intellectuals in the European metropolis trying to stay ahead of the scene.

When meeting an Arab poet or painter in Amsterdam there was sadness in their eyes, the sadness of somebody who was allowed in, but forgotten, an orphan of history, neither here nor there and not permitted by the intellectual status quo to find a way out. Most of them gave into this brutal bargain: I give you permission to stay, in exchange you will tell me sad songs of your mother country.

There was something immensely attractive about these meetings. When the East met the West, the Arab painter wanted to talk about the politics surrounding his work, while the spectator wanted something exotic, perhaps to hear the painter recite a poem about the painting in a strange language. Yes, there was dialogue, but a hasty one, full of misunderstanding. And the ones who understood this, they became numb. Meanwhile in Brussels, capital of the European Union, meetings were being held to discuss creative ideas about closing the border to the south. The big project was to tap the influx of immigrant workers from the new EU members in the East, while stimulating a slow but steady amnesia about the neighbouring countries in the Mediterranean. The sea could be used as a new wall. Lampedusa the new Berlin.

Intellectuals had nothing more to lose in the West

But 9/11 changed all this. The West became a chilly place for the Arab intellectual: not willing to give up his complex position on the involvement of the West in the Middle East, or his views on terrorism and the Arab regimes, he became a pariah, somebody who was going to be neglected in a new world order that was heralded by the slogans 'Smoking them out of their holes' and 'You are either with us or against us'. So many intellectuals, in deep shock at what happened in New York, saw events in the broader context of the West's involvement in the East and vice-versa. The terrorist attacks didn't happen out of the blue – though I remember that 9/11 as a clear blue day – but had their roots in the way the West had been wheeling and dealing with the regimes of the Middle East and the Arab world.

Now, with bigotry and anti-Muslim sentiments on the rise, many of them, young and angry, deep thinking and unfulfilled, decided they had nothing more to lose in the West and returned to Cairo, Casablanca, Beirut and Damascus, Jerusalem too. They brought with them what they had understood and seen in the metropolis of London and New York, their networks and deep knowledge of the ironies of history, and worked their way into their own world. There, though dictatorships and censorship ruled, these intellectuals at least were not seen as terrorists or dirty Arabs. Their hometown became their West, their East was the East, a place where they, for the time being, did not exist. I deeply believe one of the aftereffects of 9/11 was the focus of young urban intellectuals on the ills and sicknesses of their own society. Their governments, brutal and cynical, nonetheless decided to turn a blind eye, because they were too busy working with the West chasing fundamentalists, handing them over to the kindergartens of Guantanamo Bay.

Cruel as it may seem, it will be a long time before the fruits of the revolution can be picked. There is just too much instability in the air, instability that the power-that-replaced-the-power will use to halt the sudden influx of progress in the region. They will do everything they can to maintain the status quo, through military power, through seeking new alliances with old enemies, through money and oil to quench the thirst for change. The demographic tide is not in favour of the old regime; the demands of the people and their method of challenging power are too complex. But in the meantime, the brutal and the cynical, the old and the power hungry, the general and the spy will do their best to create confusion.

To use the historical momentum as a pretext for a new security policy is an old strategy. But for us, observers and participants, it's advisable to keep an eye on what is coming, to keep an eye on the great moment that has been created. They say that after the spring came a chilly winter, but after winter will come spring, and maybe that will be chilly too. After an absence of any season, just the cold and freeze of totalitarian rule and contempt for human rights, we have something of a season after all. I do not want to sound like Leibniz, the German philosopher who argued that we were living in the best of worlds, a free pass for often groundless optimism, nor do I want to echo the comical warning of Candide who satirises the easygoing nativism of that viewpoint.

My travels through the Arab world, my incredible, inspiring and fruitful encounters with intellectuals, writers, grocery sellers, taxi drivers, mothers, painters, dissidents, comedians, filmmakers, sound engineers, peasants, doctors, architects, politicians, volunteers and ice-vendors, gave me a deep feeling that this great complex mosaic of identities is definitely on the move towards fulfilling its destiny. Maybe we should find something in between optimism and pessimism, a new springtime that takes into account that times are changing. Count me in.

©Abdelkader Benali
40(4): 26/35
DOI: 10.1177/0306422011429408
www.indexoncensorship.org

Abdelkader Benali is a novelist and playwright. He was born in Morocco and lives in the Netherlands. His books include *Wedding by the Sea* (Weidenfeld and Nicolson). His most recent publication, *East is West*, is a collection of essays about his travels in the Middle East

DARK MATTER

What's science got to hide?

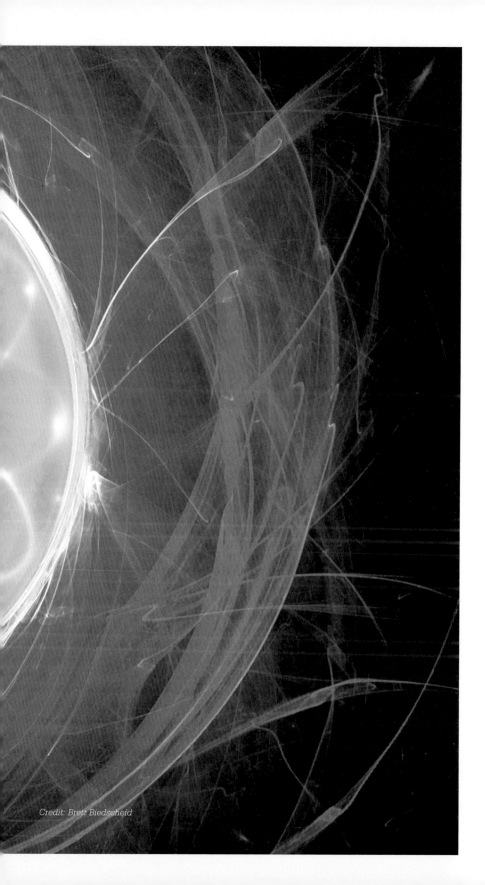
Credit: Brett Biedscheid

CHOKING DEBATE

Fear of legal action is jeopardising scientific discussion. When the open exchange of ideas is stifled we all suffer, writes **Tracey Brown**

Experiments and data ruin the best of theories: it was once deemed impossible that BSE could be transmitted from cattle to cause prion disease in humans, that the earth could be 4.5 billion years old and that many stomach ulcers are caused by bacteria, not stress. Science is a pursuit of true accounts of the natural world. It advances through troubleshooting, disputing and refuting, in open debate.

Peer-reviewed journals, rights of reply, conference papers and scientific training, faulty and uneven as they may be, are founded on the aspiration to advance ideas, share evidence and minimise the distraction of other interests, egos and dogma.

It is not just in the rarefied atmosphere of specialist research conferences and publications that we expect to see open debate about evidence. Where medical science is concerned, if doctors didn't voice reservations and medical publishers air disputes, we would have good reason to accuse them of being irresponsible. They would be failing patients. We expect that when medical regulators determine whether a medicine should be licensed, or when Home Office officials review the categorisation of a recreational drug, they have access to the full range of what is known about it – research results, records, expert opinions.

It is only in recent decades that we have come to expect scientific debates to be routinely shared with the wider public. Traditionally, public communication about science tended to be limited to 'diffusing the knowledge … of useful mechanical inventions and improvements', as the founders of the Royal Institution put it in 1799, and it has taken a concerted effort to persuade scientists and research organisations of the need to communicate evidence. Multiple vaccines, use of genetic modification, stem cell treatments, the consequences of climate change, and fears about radiation were just some of the issues that cried out for more public discussion of evidence. And now that is what we expect. Since the BSE crisis there has also been greater recognition in government of the need for independent scientific advice, and new rules require this to be open to public scrutiny.

Sense About Science, the organisation for which I work, has spent much of the past decade urging scientists to address pseudo-science and misrepresentation of evidence publicly, instead of grumbling in private, and urging the public to ask for evidence. Others have successfully pushed for more transparency, particularly around the use of science in policy-making, and scientific journals have sought more systematic declarations of competing interests.

Here the good part of the story ends. While scientific evidence is being more clearly expressed and shared, we are also becoming increasingly aware of the forces that suppress open debates about it. The expansion of science communication has been met by efforts to close down inconvenient evidence – through commercial pressure, intimidation, vandalism of research, sackings and threats of court proceedings. The value of scientific evidence in policy-making may now be recognised, but it seems to have brought with it increased political attempts to suborn or silence that evidence.

Professor David Nutt, the former chair of the UK government's Advisory Council on the Misuse of Drugs (ACMD), learned this to his cost in the autumn of 2009, when his views that LSD, ecstasy and cannabis were less harmful than alcohol and tobacco were published, causing a storm in the British media. He was sacked by the then home secretary, Alan Johnson. Many scientists involved in drug research saw his dismissal as sadly consistent with the government's continued attempts to get the scientific view on drug harms to match its press releases rather than the data.

Yet Nutt might consider himself lucky. In the months leading up to April 2009, a region of central Italy had seen an increase in seismic activity. In the face of several false alarms, seismologists advising the Italian government through its Major Hazards Committee met to review the evidence. They concluded that there was no reliable predictor of earthquakes and, despite the small-magnitude events in the region, the probability of a major quake remained low. Then, on 6 April, the city of L'Aquila, and several towns nearby, were struck by a devastating quake that killed more than 300 people and destroyed 20,000 buildings. No one has disputed the seismologists' conclusion that it was impossible to predict such an event, but the Italian government's response was to put them on trial for manslaughter.

In the same year, a scientist in Peru, who is an advocate of GM, was arrested for defamation following his public criticism of a report by a fellow Peruvian scientist on the genetic modification of crops. It was also in 2009 that civil libel actions and threats against scientists and medics in the English courts began to emerge.

The government's response was to put them on trial

Many people will be aware of the case of the science writer Simon Singh, who was sued by the British Chiropractic Association for his critical comments in the *Guardian* about the lack of evidence for claims by chiropractors that they could treat infant conditions such as ear infections. Many will also know that his appeals against the meaning given to his words by the judge were eventually successful, making him one of relatively few defendants to win a libel case. It cost Singh £200,000 and 18 anxious months just to reach that 'early' resolution. Singh will not recover all of these costs and he will never recover the hundreds of hours spent preparing legal documents and correspondence on every aspect of his short article. A prolific popular science author, he wrote no further books in that time.

Eighteen months is quite quick for a libel action, though. A case brought against the British cardiologist, Peter Wilmshurst, by the now

Protesters demand the reinstatement of former government drugs advisor
Professor David Nutt, Downing Street, London, 7 November 2009
Credit: Dominic Lipinski/PA Wire

defunct US implant manufacturer NMT Medical, continued for almost four years and only came to an end very recently because the company collapsed. Dr Wilmshurst was sued for making comments at an American cardiology conference, to a Canadian writer, about a clinical trial of a heart device in which he had been a principal investigator. He had refused to put his name to a paper publishing the results in a clinical journal because he felt that it overstated the benefits and understated the risks of the procedure. The US company sued him in England. After he had refused other inducements to agree to the company's interpretation, and talked publicly about his case, they sued him again. He and his lawyers incurred around £300,000 in costs and yet never got any further than dealing with the preliminary legal exchanges. No statements were served, no experts reported, and it was only at the start of 2011 that NMT was forced to pay money into court as security for costs – money which, now the company is defunct, will not meet the bill so far.

It might be tempting to think that courts, used to handling evidence, would throw light on disputes about science. They are liable to have the opposite effect. The defensiveness that they induce, with selective presentation of evidence to fit the case being made, stands in complete opposition to the open presentation of evidence and willingness to revise ideas that are essential to advance scientific debate. Had Dr Wilmshurst's case eventually come to court, we may have learned more about the risks and benefits of NMT's device or we may have learned nothing, and it is highly unlikely that a cardiologist anywhere would have been following the legal debate to ascertain the safety of the device for patients. It was equally unlikely that climate science would have been advanced by the trial threatened by the US Chamber of Commerce two years ago, where it envisaged a judge presiding over witnesses to pronounce on whether humans are warming the planet in what it billed as 'the Scopes monkey trial of the 21st century' (John Scopes was a teacher in the 1920s at the centre of a case which threw light only on the law regarding teaching evolution in American schools and no light at all on the science of evolution; see pp. 87–98).

More importantly, the damage to scientific debate from intimidation and court actions is not confined to the scientists being sued, bad as that is. The very threat of the libel laws in England means robust criticism brings a risk of ruin that is chilling scientific and medical debates more widely. The last government's plans to roll out a new lie detector for pension and benefit claimants were developed in the absence of a critical review by language experts, because a libel threat from the lie detector's manufacturer had caused the

Aftermath of the earthquake in L'Aqila, Italy, which struck on 6 April 2009
Credit: Action Press/Rex Features

journal to withdraw its paper. The consumer magazine *Which?* struggles against legal threats, sometimes unsuccessfully, in order to discuss the safety of products. Science journals confess that their news and comment writers do not investigate many stories of fraud or misconduct because they would risk being bankrupted by a libel action before they ever got to defend themselves in court.

The consequence is that we are now reading or hearing only the sanitised, 'legalled' part of many stories, and not hearing about some issues at all. That is particularly alarming when it comes to subjects such as a clinic offering pseudo-scientific advice about nutrient deficiencies to parents of autistic children, which no one will report because the clinic's owner is a notorious litigant, or the unwillingness of researchers to speak out when they think that funders misrepresent data from a clinical trial, since Wilmshurst was sued for doing so. As Fiona Godlee, the editor-in-chief of the *British Medical Journal*, wrote in 2009: 'Weak science sheltered from criticism by officious laws means bad medicine.'

Dr Wilmshurst felt he didn't have a choice when faced with libel action. As a doctor registered with the General Medical Council, he is obliged to act in the best interests of patients rather than in fear of his own financial security. A radiology professor faced the same obligation in a case brought (and dropped) by the US company GE Healthcare, when he criticised the contrast agent used in medical scans. The medical writer Ben Goldacre fought an action by a German vitamin salesman because the alternative would have been to fall silent about the man's promotion of vitamins as an HIV medication in Africa.

We heard about these cases because the scientists involved fought back. Many can't and don't. Others look at what happened to Nutt, the Italian seismologists or Goldacre and decide to take no chances in the public domain. If Simon Singh's case is what 'winning' amounts to, it is not surprising that the threat of such a libel action chills others into silence and self-censorship. What will be the impact on the next person who contemplates voicing concerns about a medical device or contradicts evidence that underpins government policy? What will happen the next time the Italian government tries to convene a disaster management review? And we already know from the resignations from the ACMD after Nutt's sacking that securing independent scientific advice on drug policy has become more difficult.

While we press for greater communication of evidence in scientific discussions, we are facing a situation where the obligation to speak up is frequently overwhelmed by attempts to suppress that evidence. Perhaps these attempts are the consequence of the more open communication of science and the disruption that can cause to settled thinking and authority. Whatever the reason, as debates disappear behind the doors of Whitehall, the lab and the court room, we need to defend open scientific discussion.

Some have suggested that perhaps science is a special case for free speech. If it is, it is not by virtue of being a genteel practice of exchanging polite, balanced views in which all the evidence has been accumulated before a public pronouncement is made. It might be reasonably well disciplined and organised, but scientific debate is just as likely to be rude, unfair and one-sided. Every Friday at all major hospitals, Grand Rounds take place, in which consultants pick over and criticise the treatment of a case, and in which the reputations of those concerned are firmly secondary to the aim of improving knowledge and patient care. In most scientific journals the correspondence pages carry critical disputes about the conclusions of recent research papers, mortifying to some researchers but necessary to advancing knowledge in the field.

Science is not an esoteric category of speech. Rather, what science does is most clearly articulate the collaborative open exchange that is needed in the pursuit of a true picture of our world. It brings into sharp relief the dangers of suppression and it reminds us, as the English philosopher Thomas Hobbes wrote in 1651, at the birth of scientific inquiry, that: 'True and False are attributes of speech, not of things. And where speech is not, there is neither Truth nor Falsehood.' ❑

© Tracey Brown
40(4): 40/47
DOI: 10.1177/0306422011427625
www.indexoncensorship.org

Tracey Brown is managing director of Sense About Science (www.senseaboutscience.org)

DATA TRAP

Chinese activists are pushing for transparency on the environment. **Sam Geall** reports

'Two wells at a Bohai oilfield have been leaking for two days. I hope the leaks are controlled and pollution prevented.' Users of China's Sina Weibo microblogging site (similar to Twitter, which is blocked in China) read this short post on 21 June 2011. It is unclear who wrote it, thanks in part to the government censors who deleted the message, but Chinese bloggers believe it came from a whistleblower at China National Offshore Oil Corporation (CNOOC), the state-owned company that forms half of a joint venture with US oil giant ConocoPhillips at the Penglai 19-3 oilfield in the Bohai Sea, the innermost bay of the Yellow Sea, between north-eastern China and the Korean Peninsula.

Oil and drilling fluid had spilled into the already murky water. The size of the leak eventually reached about 2,500 barrels, according to state media, polluting around 4,250 square kilometres of sea. Fishermen in Hebei Province blamed the spill for the deaths of huge numbers of scallops, only a year after a pipeline explosion in the Yellow Sea caused the country's worst ever oil leak and devastated the shellfish industry. Zhao Zhangyuan, a retired researcher at the Chinese Research Academy of Environmental Sciences, who estimates that the leak was far larger than the figures cited, recently told a public forum in Beijing that the Bohai's fragile ecology is close to collapse and that continued development could cause it to 'become a dead sea'.

Public controversy over the leak, however, was not confined to the environmental damage it caused. Outrage soon began to swell about secrecy and the lack of accountability and public oversight in China. After that lone microblogger had sounded the alarm, Chinese environmentalists and journalists started to ask questions, but CNOOC and China's State Oceanic Administration (SOA) remained tight-lipped. (It later turned out that the microblog referred to an accident that had happened on 17 June, but another leak had also occurred 13 days earlier, and neither the SOA nor the company had made this information public.)

The pressure continued to build: the outspoken, Guangzhou-based, weekly newspaper *Southern Weekend* broke the story in print at the end of June; though without official confirmation or access to data, the report mainly focused on fears of a cover-up. Chinese green NGOs sent open letters and even chartered a boat to survey the damage themselves. Commentators asked whether the Chinese government would similarly hide news of an accident at one of the many new nuclear reactors it plans to build. Finally, the SOA confirmed the accident on 5 July, a full month after the first leak.

Outrage soon began to swell about secrecy

Then, on 12 July, another leak occurred at a different CNOOC oilfield in the Bohai Sea. But this time the response was different: the SOA announced the small leak and the next day ordered the company to cease operations and to make information about the accident available to the public. It was a breakthrough for transparency in China. Green activist Ma Jun, author of the seminal book *China's Water Crisis* and founder of the Beijing-based NGO the Institute of Public and Environmental Affairs (IPE), wrote that it was 'the first time a government department has urged a polluting company to disclose information on an incident of this kind'. It meant 'finally, the publication of environmental information has moved from being a public and media desire to a government requirement'.

There is good evidence that being open with environmental information is a cost-effective method for pollution control that can harness social participation and public pressure to reduce environmental hazards, often more effectively than top-down measures such as tightening emissions standards. The lack of open information in China has long been an impediment for environmental researchers, journalists and concerned citizens. For nine days in July 2010, for example, Zijin Mining managed to conceal from the central authorities and the public a massive wastewater leak from one of its copper mines into the Ting River in Fujian Province, southern China, that killed more than 1,500 tonnes of fish. A month after the disaster, villagers told the Southern Metropolis Daily that while they used to catch turtles, grouper, beardfish and eels in the river, now it was mostly dead. Eating what you caught was said to be 'as dangerous as taking poison'.

Last year, my organisation, chinadialogue, tried to conduct an investigation in the city of Dongguan, a manufacturing hub in southern China's Pearl River Delta that is thought to have high rates of occupational- and pollution-related diseases. Our researchers were continually rebuffed. Time and again, requests for interviews were refused; the environmental protection bureau, the local hospital, oncologists and environmental scientists all declined to speak to us. Even the proceedings of public academic conferences on environmental medicine were said to be confidential. One soil expert who agreed to an interview had to consult government officials first, who told him not to make any data available to the researchers.

It might be surprising then to learn that in 2008 the Chinese government introduced legislation not dissimilar to the UK's Freedom of Information Act: the Regulations of the People's Republic of China on Open Government Information. Even if the spirit of these regulations hadn't convinced officials in Dongguan, Article 1 clearly states that the purpose of the regulations is to 'ensure that citizens, legal persons and other organisations obtain government information in accordance with the law, enhance transparency of the work of government, promote administration in accordance with the law, and bring into full play the role of government information in serving the people's production and livelihood and their economic and social activities'.

The regulations, issued by China's State Council – an executive body chaired by Premier Wen Jiabao, which co-ordinates government ministries and helps to bind the Chinese Communist Party (CCP) with the central

Residents from Harbin, north-east China queue for water after the city's water system was closed as a result of a chemical spill in the Songhua River, 26 November 2005
Credit: Lou Linwei/Rex Features

government, as well as, in effect, extending the regulations downward to provincial and local governments – establish two basic types of open government information. First, that which should be proactively disseminated by government agencies at various levels – for example, on their official websites – which includes reports on 'financial budgets and final accounts'; emergency plans and early-warning information 'against sudden public events'; and information 'on the supervision and inspection of environmental protection, public health, safe production, food and drugs, and product quality'. Second, that which should be disclosed in response to requests from the public, usually free of charge (although the requester has to cover the costs of producing the information), within 15 to 30 days. The regulations outline a bureaucratic infrastructure for this system, including that 'administrative organs' should designate an office 'to be responsible for the daily work of open government information' and a requirement that annual reports on open government information should be published by 'administrative organs at all levels'.

As with similar legislation in other countries, there is a clause that stipulates the exemptions from disclosure – Article 8: 'The government information disclosed by administrative organs may not endanger state security, public security, economic security and social stability.'

There is also Article 17, which states that if other laws or regulations 'have different provisions on the scope of authorisation to disclose government information, those provisions shall be followed'. This means that other laws, such as the state secrets law – which is frequently used in China, not only to keep controversial information from public view, but also as a means of silencing individuals critical of the government – can trump the regulations.

The introduction of these regulations was preceded by a period of experimentation, which included local pilots and several years of research by the Chinese Academy of Social Sciences, an influential think-tank. Many Chinese government officials, particularly at the centre, believe there are benefits to greater transparency, for example, to help keep tabs on inefficiency and local corruption (an official from the State Council told reporters that the regulations would 'help curb corruption at its source, largely reducing its occurrence'). However, in the hands of China's grassroots environmentalists, it could be a powerful tool to hold polluters to account.

Environmental policy is a more tolerated sphere for public participation than many others in China, and although others have used the regulations – Chinese Aids campaigners, for example, have requested information about policies on protecting HIV/Aids sufferers – it is not surprising that the first government department to implement the national regulations as a more specific decree was the Ministry of Environmental Protection (MEP), a relatively weak body that has for a long time encouraged civil society and media oversight of environmental regulations to make up for lax enforcement by local governments that frequently prioritise economic growth over curbing pollution. The result was the Environmental Information Disclosure Decree, which requires, for example, that enterprises identified as 'major industrial polluters' should disclose and report emissions data within 30 days of a request from the public. It also sets out guidelines for the proactive disclosure of 17 types of government-held environmental information. It is on these latter measures that there has been the most progress. The website of Beijing's municipal environmental protection bureau, for example, clearly discloses these 17 categories of information, including environmental laws, regulations, standards and administrative permits.

However, a report by free-expression campaigners Article 19, found that the Beijing bureau, despite its comprehensive website, was poor at responding to requests for information from the public. According to the report's author Amy Sim: 'A lot of officials interpret [the regulations]: as long as it's not within the 17 types of proactive disclosure, they will not disclose.' Reading the study, it's clear that more sensitive information of relevance to campaigners – for example on the disposal and discharge of hazardous waste – is still very difficult to obtain. Alex Wang, a Chinese environmental law expert at the University of California, Berkeley, said: 'China has made great strides in environmental disclosure in recent years, but right now the types of information that are most critical to uncovering environmental problems – emissions data, records of violations, environmental impact assessment reports – are still difficult, if not impossible, for the public to obtain.'

But with these regulations in place, on what grounds is sensitive information still being withheld? Speaking at a seminar in April, Wang Canfa, director of Beijing's Centre for Legal Assistance to Pollution Victims, said: 'Although the regulations list 17 types of information that should be disclosed and only one short clause on exemptions, that one short clause has become a catch-all.' He referred here to Article 8, the exemption clause in the national regulations regarding national security and social stability, which also applies to the environmental decree.

An official told them the information was 'confidential'

Open information legislation across the world contains similar exemptions. The extent to which a government relies upon these can give a good indication of its commitment to its own openness policy. But in China the situation is a little more complicated. In an authoritarian country you might expect to see 'state security, public security, economic security and social stability' relied on frequently as grounds to refuse requests for information. But although refusals from Chinese government agencies to release information are frequent, in her study of environmental information requests Sim discovered that such justifications were not cited as much as other explanations that, in fact, had no legal basis whatsoever. The grounds for rejection, she found, were generally 'not very clear': many officials replied that the information was simply 'inconvenient to disclose' or that it was 'liable to be sensationalised by the media'. As with much regulation in China, the existence of the legislation – which, on the books, looks to be in line with international norms – doesn't mean that it is being effectively, consistently or accurately enforced.

The press in China has taken an active interest in the poor implementation of transparency rules. In 2009, it became headline news in the country when two journalists from the government news agency Xinhua were stopped from photographing documents listing pollution violators, information that the authorities are supposed to disclose, at a provincial government meeting in Heilongjiang, north-east China. (It was this province that was most affected in 2005, when a series of explosions at a petrochemical plant created an 80-kilometre long toxic slick in the Songhua River. The State Environmental Protection Administration, the predecessor of the MEP, only admitted the serious pollution of the river ten days after the explosion and one day after water was cut off in the provincial capital of Harbin.) When an official told them the information was 'confidential' and the media already had 'enough' information about pollution, the reporters walked out of the meeting in protest – a gesture that earned them widespread sympathy from Chinese media commentators.

However, despite their interest in the implementation of the regulations, Chinese journalists have not made much use of the legislation itself. Last year I conducted a study, involving questionnaires and in-depth interviews with reporters, about the coverage of climate change in the Chinese media. Asked about the greatest obstacle to their reporting, many journalists replied that it was the lack of official transparency. For example, one said: 'Information is not transparent enough. The government contacts the media only when the government needs to express something in the media, but the government rarely grants interview requests and officials often just speak in official language.'

But surprisingly, few of the journalists that I interviewed were aware that open information laws existed in China. None had used them to request information. In early 2009, *Southern Weekend* published on its website an environmental impact assessment, obtained using open government information laws, which approved the construction of a controversial petrochemical plant in Fujian Province. But such cases are very rare. The *Press Freedom Index*, published by Reporters Without Borders, last year placed China in its bottom ten countries: at 171 of 178 nations. Watchdog journalism is on the rise in China, especially in local newspapers and regarding

A 'functionally extinct' rare freshwater finless porpoise found only in the Yangtze River
Credit: Richard Jones/Rex Features

environmental issues, but the evidence suggests that the press is still hob-
bled by tight restrictions and a powerful censorship apparatus.

This may help to explain why pressure for open information has come
not as often from the press as from former journalists, who choose to work
instead with the country's burgeoning civil society organisations. This not
only includes Ma Jun, who used to write for the *South China Morning Post*,
but also the *Guangming Daily* journalist Feng Yongfeng, one of the activists
who sailed out to the Bohai spill and founder of the NGO Green Beagle (named
after the ship that took Charles Darwin on his famous voyage), which gath-
ers together citizen journalists and amateur naturalists to explore the hidden
waterways of Beijing; or Xi Zhinong, a cameraman who sparked a popular
campaign against wildlife habitat destruction in Yunnan, south-west China.

The country's oldest environmental NGO is Friends of Nature (FON). It has
been campaigning since 2009 for the government to disclose information about
its plan to move the boundaries of a protected area for rare and endangered fish

species on the Yangtze River, a decision that it suspects is intended to make way for the planned Xiaonanhai dam project, near the city of Chongqing in southwest China. This boundary change 'basically means a death sentence for these endangered species', said Chang Cheng, a Beijing-based campaigner for FON. The species include the Chinese paddlefish and the Yangtze sturgeon, a so-called 'living fossil' that has survived for some 140 million years, since the time of the dinosaurs. (In 2006, another ancient creature from the Yangtze River was declared 'functionally extinct': the Baiji, a freshwater dolphin that had been living exclusively in that river for the past 20 million years.)

Using open government information laws, FON requested a copy of the government's on-site investigation report and the declaration of the boundary change, which includes an impact assessment. But the Ministry of Agriculture refused these on the grounds that 'procedural' data is not covered by transparency legislation. Chang told me in an email: 'This is like a "Catch-22" situation for the public who wish to supervise and participate in the government's decision-making.' He has a point: if the government isn't willing to disclose how its decisions are made, and if its procedures aren't being correctly followed, it's difficult to see how freedom of information can be used to hold the government to account at any time other than after the event. Or to put it another way – it won't be much help to find out that procedures were carried out incorrectly after the Yangtze sturgeon is declared extinct. The green group has teamed up with the China University of Political Science and Law to demand an administrative review that challenges the legality of this 'Catch-22' situation. They are still awaiting the result.

More than any other organisation, IPE, Ma Jun's green group, has made extensive use of open government information to build the country's first publicly accessible online databases of water and air pollution; it also uses the information to monitor the progress of government transparency itself, with regular reports including the *Pollution Information Transparency Index* and the *Air Quality Transparency Index*, which compare the availability of environmental information in cities across China, fostering a sense of competition between municipalities and keeping note of broad trends and specific violations. As a result, IPE has not only helped citizens to gain more accurate and timely information about pollution incidents and to strengthen environmental enforcement, but also has found an effective, innovative way to campaign for greater freedom of information and public participation.

The state of open government information reflects the delicate balancing act that defines governance in China today: between pressure for greater openness, public oversight and even grassroots democracy, while maintaining stability (or 'harmony') through high rates of economic growth, enhancing 'social management' and safeguarding the unchallenged political authority of the CCP. Yet there is hope in the dynamic way that the public has taken up the greater openness of government information in China. Even if the press has yet to embrace the regulations, grassroots activists have pushed forward transparency for the benefit of Chinese citizens. But for now, the country is far from its fifth-century poet Xie Lingyun's vision of 'deep pools of bright-hued fish' – writing at a time when a coherent notion of the environment first emerged in Chinese culture. Today, there is not only an oil sheen on the Bohai Sea and the extinction of prehistoric river species to contemplate, but also the murky culture of censorship and obfuscation faced by the country's defenders of the natural world. ❒

©Sam Geall
40(4): 48/58
DOI: 10.1177/0306422011427642
www.indexoncensorship.org

Sam Geall is deputy editor of chinadialogue, a bilingual website and journal dedicated to open debate about all environmental issues. He lives in London and tweets as @samgeall

SECRET TRIALS

Studies to test the safety and efficacy of drugs and medical devises are too often never made public, putting lives at risk. **Deborah Cohen** reports

Transparency is at the heart of medical science. Every day decisions are made about when to stop and start treatment and how best to invest large sums of money in ways to protect the public from disease. All these rely on knowing as much as possible about the benefits compared to the risks of action or inaction.

No medical treatment is perfect or suitable for everyone – that's why balancing risks and benefits is crucial. But healthcare is big business; it's where science meets big money and not all research evidence makes it into the public domain – specifically into medical journals where doctors and academics glean their information.

Medical history is replete with examples of the benefits of a treatment being overhyped and potentially serious side-effects being buried, leading to poor decisions. This wastes public money and can cost lives.

Take the case of the drug lorcainide, used to regulate the heartbeat during a heart attack. In the early 80s, researchers in Nottingham carried out a study of the drug in 95 people using a method known as a randomised control trial. They noticed that nine out of the 48 people taking the drug died, compared to only one out of 47 who got a sugar pill, or placebo, instead.

Plates of bacteria are analysed as part of research into antibiotics
Credit: Geoff Tompkinson/Science Photo Library

At the time, the researchers thought that the high number of deaths in those given lorcainide might have been due to chance rather than the drug itself. For commercial reasons, the drug was not developed any further and the results of the trial were never published. However other, similar, heart drugs did make it onto the market and were widely used. But they too had serious safety problems and many were withdrawn.

According to Sir Iain Chalmers, a long-standing champion of transparency in medical research, the lorcainide trial might have been an early warning of trouble ahead for these other heart drugs. At the peak of their use in the late 80s, these medicines are estimated to have caused between 20,000 and 70,000 premature deaths every year in the US alone.

This is a particularly stark example of what might happen when critical evidence remains unavailable to doctors and researchers. Even when individual drugs do make it onto the market and have overcome the regulatory hurdles, information about their risks and benefits might well be hard to come by.

In western countries, legislation dictates that companies have to provide regulators with a thorough scientific dossier on all trials conducted on a drug so the data can be scrutinised before the drug is allowed onto the market. They are then required to do follow-up studies looking at any adverse reactions that might not have been picked up in the pre-market research. They must inform the authorities about what they find.

Many companies, however, have been reprimanded – mainly in the US courts – for hiding troubling side-effects of drugs, including: anti-depressants, such as Seroxat (known as Paxil in the US; generic name paroxetine) and painkillers, such as Vioxx (rofecoxib).

But it's not always the companies which are unforthcoming about safety concerns; the regulators have dragged their feet too. Last year, the diabetes drug Avandia (rosiglitazone) was suspended from the market in Europe and severely restricted in the US because of an increased risk of heart problems. But this was long after both the manufacturer, GlaxoSmithKline (GSK), and the US regulator had reason to suspect an increase in serious side-effects.

Rather than the regulators – whose remit is to protect the public – it was the actions of the then New York attorney general, Eliot Spitzer, in a 2004 court case of GSK's Seroxat, that led to the side-effects of Avandia coming to public attention. As part of a settlement with the state over its hiding of data on heightened suicide risk in teenagers who took the drug, GSK agreed to post results from its recent clinical studies on a website. And this included studies of the drug Avandia, many of which had been unpublished until then.

Three years later, Dr Steven Nissen, chairman of cardiovascular medicine at the high-profile Cleveland Clinic in the US, decided to analyse all the studies of Avandia on the website. Using a research method called meta-analysis, he pooled all the results together to see what they said overall. He found that the risk of having heart problems in people with diabetes who took the drug rose by 43 per cent compared to those who had diabetes and did not take it.

The following years entailed investigations into GSK's conduct by the US Senate; intense deliberations by national drug regulators; questions about how we regulate medicine; and now pending class actions. But what really broke the case open was enforced transparency.

'It's important to realise what an important role publicly available trial results data played in the rosiglitazone story', said Jerry Avorn, professor of medicine at Harvard Medical School.

During an investigation in collaboration with BBC's *Panorama* in September 2010, the *BMJ* looked into the different drug regulators' attitudes towards transparency. In the US, the Food and Drug Administration's (FDA) advisory committee discussions are held in public in front of the national press. Most of the relevant scientific documents are made available on a website in advance. Before the deliberations start, each panellist is required to declare any conflicts of interest in line with US legislation to increase transparency.

But gaining an overall perspective of discussions within the European and UK regulators was far trickier. The BMJ attempted to speak to people who had sat on panels for them both, but they were bound by confidentiality clauses. Nor would Europe's regulator release the names of the members of the scientific advisory group discussing the drug under the Freedom of Information Act (FOIA).

Doctors and the public in the UK had not been told that the national regulator had voted unanimously to take Avandia off the market several months before the European agency came to the same decision. If the European vote had gone the other way, who knows if the views of the UK's panel would ever have been revealed.

Advisers had concerns about side-effects from the outset

Some say that open discussions and more transparency do not necessarily lead to better decisions. But documents obtained from the European regulators under the FOIA showed that advisers had concerns about Avandia's side-effects from the outset. And knowing about these could have lent support to other academics who were 'intimidated' by the company, according to a 2007 report by the US Senate Finance Committee.

In 1999, when the drug was first licensed, Dr John Buse, a professor of medicine at the University of North Carolina who specialises in diabetes, told attendees of academic meetings that he was concerned that while Avandia lowered blood sugar, it also caused an increased risk of heart problems.

Concerned about the effects that his comments would have on their drug that had been touted for blockbuster status, executives at GSK (then SmithKline Beecham) devised 'what appears to be an orchestrated plan to stifle his opinion', the Senate Finance Committee report stated – in the light of internal company documents it had seen.

Food and Drug Administration officers review an experimental
drug manufactured by Merck, Maryland, USA, 12 April 2007
Credit: Stephanie Kuykendal/Bloomberg/Getty

The report goes on to state that GSK executives labelled Buse a 'renegade' and silenced his concerns about Avandia by complaining to his superiors and threatening a lawsuit. GSK prepared and required Buse to sign a letter claiming that he was no longer worried about cardiovascular risks associated with Avandia. Then, after he signed the letter, GSK officials began referring to it as Buse's 'retraction letter' to curry favour with a financial consulting company that was evaluating GSK's products for investors. GSK has denied all allegations in the report, describing them as 'absolutely false'.

Years later, Buse wrote a private email to a colleague detailing the incident with GSK: 'I was certainly intimidated by them. … It makes me embarrassed to have caved in several years ago.'

Meanwhile, over on the other side of the Atlantic, EU drug agencies were drawing similar conclusions that the drug increased the risk of heart problems during their premarket discussions. In March 2000, Buse sent a letter to the FDA, saying Avandia might raise patients' risk of heart attacks, and he criticised the company's marketing, saying it employed 'blatant selective manipulation of data' to overstate the drug's benefits and understate its risks. Doctors may not have prescribed the drug if they had known from the outset there were issues around its safety.

But data transparency doesn't just mean exposing harm done, it can also help to establish how well something works – and that reported benefits aren't just hype. Major international decisions are made on how best to tackle impending health crises based on how well a medical invention works as reported in journals, for example the UK government's decision to stockpile the influenza drug Tamiflu.

Back in 2009, during the swine flu pandemic, the internationally respected Cochrane Collaboration, a network of independent academics, was commissioned by the NHS to look at the evidence about the benefits and risks of using Tamiflu – a drug the UK had spent around £500m on to treat all those infected in the outbreak.

The academics, led by Christopher Del Mar at Bond University in Australia, scoured the medical literature to find all the different relevant studies of the drug to pool together all the results to see what they said. They were also aware that there had been reports of suicides in Japan – the biggest consumers of Tamiflu – and they wanted to find out more.

But when they went about surveying the medical literature, not all of the trials they knew existed about the effects of the drug in healthy people appeared in the medical press. To fairly reflect the evidence, they needed to know exactly what all trials said. But they couldn't access all the data they needed – the majority of trials were unpublished. This included the biggest, and therefore arguably the most important, trial conducted.

The UK government at the time had based its decision to stockpile Tamiflu in such large quantities on one particular piece of research published in 2003. This paper showed the dramatic benefits of giving Tamiflu to healthy people who got the flu and not just those who were at particular risk of getting sick. It claimed that the drug reduced the number of people taken to hospital with the flu by a half and reduced serious complications by around the same amount. Little wonder that health officials, concerned about the strain on the NHS, stockpiled the red and yellow pills in such vast quantities.

But this piece of research was funded by the drug's manufacturer, Roche. It relied upon eight unpublished studies, each given code names, and used the company's own statisticians to draw conclusions about the data. The two independent researchers named on the paper – who are supposed to be accountable for the content of the research – could not produce the unpublished studies when the Cochrane Collaboration asked them.

Medical research relies heavily on the ability to replicate the findings of another piece of research. This helps to show that a finding wasn't fraudulent or simply due to chance.

But the Cochrane Collaboration couldn't replicate the 2003 findings. Its calculations based on the publicly available papers were at odds with the claims made and it needed to see the unpublished studies, so it turned to the company.

Despite asking Roche repeatedly for the full complement of research documents showing that Tamiflu would stop so many healthy people from going into hospital, the whole set were never forthcoming. What it did provide was limited in detail and not what the Cochrane Collaboration needed. Roche did nothing illegal – it is its commercial information. But its commercial information has huge repercussions for public health spend – both in terms of direct costs of the drug and its distribution, but also on what economists call the opportunity costs. Half a billion spent on Tamiflu is half a billion not spent on some other wonder drug.

Del Mar and his team were left to wonder if these bold claims really did stack up – and if the unpublished trials really were the best of the lot, why were they unpublished?

What should have been a straightforward exercise to confirm the evidence base for current policy and practice became instead a complex investigation involving the Cochrane Collaboration, the *BMJ* and *Channel 4 News*. Not only did this unmask the extent of unpublished data, it found that the person who actually wrote some of the journal papers was never credited – known in the trade as ghostwriting.

This is not the benign undertaking it is in celebrity autobiographies. Commercial medical writing firms team up with drug companies to draft a series of academic papers aimed at medical journals to promote a carefully crafted message. In the case of Tamiflu, it was that the drug helps to reduce serious complications.

The lead investigator author who was named on the biggest trial – which was unpublished – said that he couldn't remember ever having participated in the trial when the *BMJ/Channel 4 News* asked him. And the investigation revealed that documents submitted to Nice (the National Institute for Health and Clinical Excellence) show different investigator names appended to the key Tamiflu trials at different points – nowhere is it totally clear who took overall responsibility for all of the studies.

In a later twist, an investigation the *BMJ* conducted with the Bureau of Investigative Journalism revealed that experts who had been paid to promote Tamiflu were also authors of influential World Health Organisation (WHO) guidance on the treatment and prevention of pandemic flu. Nowhere were their conflicts of interest made public, despite the WHO having a specific policy to exclude those with such major competing interests from crafting guidelines. And when the scientific evidence pointed to a serious global outbreak of swine flu in early 2009, the WHO pulled together an international expert panel called the Emergency Committee. Keeping up the trend of opacity that had been a recurrent feature of pandemic planning, the committee executed its decisions – which the former health secretary, Alan Johnson, said would lead to 'costly and risky' repercussions – behind closed doors in Geneva. An internal WHO investigation conducted by Harvey Fineberg, president of the US Institute of Medicine, criticised the lack of transparency and timely disclosure of conflicts of interest in May last year.

'The public pay for the drug, the public should have access'

After an inauspicious start – with experts from within the US regulatory agency saying the benefits of healthy people taking the drug were marginal at the outset – Tamiflu sales sky-rocketed. This, coupled with a mild strain of flu and an abject lack of transparency, allowed conspiracy theories to ferment that alleged the WHO was in league with big pharma and had fostered fears of a pandemic in order to boost sales of drugs. And with blogosphere rumours abounding, not only has the WHO's reputation taken a hit, scepticism might well accompany future warnings of serious flu outbreaks.

Yet again the role of the regulators comes into the spotlight. Roche said that it had supplied all the required data to US and EU regulatory authorities. Only after five months of chasing drug regulators with FOI requests, asking for the full study reports of trials that Roche submitted for its market approval, did the Cochrane Collaboration get some of what it asked for.

'Open access should be the default setting for drug trials once the drug is registered. The public pay for the drug, the public should have access to the facts, not sanitised versions of them', one of the Cochrane collaborators, Dr Tom Jefferson, said. He believes that drug regulators should make data accessible once a drug comes onto the market. Others suggest that the regulators should also publish the data of drugs that have failed to make it onto the market. That way the situation that happened with locainide would be avoided.

This, too, might be helpful for those charged with making decisions about which drugs health services should use, such as Nice. Writing in the *BMJ* last year, researchers from the official German drug assessment body charged with synthesising evidence on the antidepressant Edronax (generic: reboxetine) reported they had encountered serious obstacles when they tried to get unpublished clinical trial information from the drug company that held the data.

Once they were able to integrate the astounding 74 per cent of patient data that had previously been unpublished, their conclusion was damning: Edronax (reboxetine) is 'overall an ineffective and potentially harmful antidepressant'. This conclusion starkly contradicted the findings of other recent studies that pooled the data published by reputable journals.

But the amounts of data submitted to regulators can be voluminous – another reason why overstretched and underfunded drug authorities could benefit from the safeguard of publicly available data that academics could analyse. The Cochrane Collaboration is now in possession of over 24,000 pages to peruse and distil. But this kind of volume doesn't deter researchers; they are actively asking for it.

In June this year, Medtronic, a medical technology company, drew widespread criticism in the US for its alleged failure in published research papers to mention the side-effects of a spinal treatment it manufactures. Capitalising on the company's dip in public opinion, Harlan Krumholz, professor of medicine and public health at Yale University, approached Medtronic to take part in a transparency programme for industry that he had set up. He wanted access to all data it had on file – published and unpublished – to commission two independent reviews of it to see what it really said about safety.

'Industry's reputation has really dropped substantially. People are concerned. They've lost confidence and trust in these companies,' Krumholz said, adding: 'Marketing has sometimes gotten the best of the companies and there have been some episodes that have tarnished their reputation. So they are in great need to show to the public that they are really interested in the societal good and want to contribute in ways that are meaningful.'

The company obliged and described its move as 'unprecedented in the medical industry'. Needless to say, not all companies are keen on having their data analysed by independent researchers. When Krumholz first approached manufacturers asking them to allow the scientific community to vet their data when safety concerns had emerged, he was rebuffed at every turn. Nevertheless, he hopes this will change and transparency will become expected rather than simply celebrated. He hopes his scheme will make it impossible for other companies – particularly when questions are being raised about the safety of their products – to simply say that they are not going to share all the information they have that may be relevant.

But there is a broader ethical aspect to selective publication. People often participate in clinical trials because they want to help grow scientific knowledge. And the very nature of many trials means there is a level of uncertainty of what a drug or device may do. This includes any potential benefits and it also involves risks.

According to Chalmers, those who don't publish all the studies are betraying the trust of those who have volunteered themselves to medical science. 'If a patient takes part in a clinical trial – which is essentially an experiment – they are doing their service to humanity and putting themselves at the disposal of science. Unless patients are explicitly told that the results won't be published if the trial does not show what the researchers or the company want before they start the trial, there is a dereliction of duty on behalf of the researchers.'

Chalmers is uncompromising on what the fate of doctors who are complicit in the burying of bad results should be – they should face discipline that might include the loss of their right to practise medicine or conduct research. His mood reflects a growing concern about the moral duty of medical scientists to publish their results. Journal editors have railed against what they consider a distortion of the medical literature.

But for many years there has been comparative silence from organisations representing people conducting medical research. In the UK, the charge for transparency has been led by the Faculty of Pharmaceutical Medicine in London. Over a decade ago, it said: 'Pharmaceutical physicians have a particular ethical responsibility to ensure that the evidence on which doctors should make their prescribing decisions is freely available.'

In June this year, the Royal Statistical Society followed suit and released a statement saying it is 'committed to transparency in scientific and social research'. It said it is 'crucially important that the results of scientific research should be made publicly available and disseminated as widely as is practical

H1N1 influenza graffiti, Mumbai, India, 9 September 2009
Credit: Arko Datta/Reuters

in a timely fashion after completion of the scientific investigation provided that there is no conflict with any legislation on confidentiality of data'.

Chalmers is critical of organisations who represent people conducting medical research – such as the Academy of Medical Sciences and the Royal College of Physicians – which refuse to sign up to a bill of transparency.

Attempts have been made to limit a researcher's ability to hide trials that they may not want to come to light. Registers of trials sprang up. In 2005, the International Committee of Medical Journal Editors said its journals would only publish trials that were fully registered before they started – which should make trials that went missing much easier to spot. Then, in 2007, the US implemented legislation to ensure that all trials protocols are listed on a public searchable website called clinicaltrials.gov. Companies are supposed to update the information with changes or highlight when and where their research has been published. But the *BMJ* has found instances where the information on the website is out of date. And, unless someone goes through the database systematically to identify what studies have surfaced publicly, it's hard to pin down exactly what impact the register has had on publication bias.

But once again, Europe trails behind in terms of transparency. The names of the trials being conducted in the EU appear on the EudraCT database. But crucial details of the study design and where it's taking place are not on the website.

If data transparency is an issue for drugs, the opacity surrounding medical device governance is in a different league. Medical devices cover a wide range of products from adhesive bandages and syringes to heavy duty implantables, such as hip prostheses, pacemakers and stents.

Representatives of the drug industry marvel at how devices get away with a comparative lack of government and public oversight both in the US and the EU. Debates about the perceived flaws in the US system have been hammered out in public – the media weighing in on what they considered to be a failure of their regulators to protect the public adequately. Front page coverage of hip replacements failing and heart devices misfiring has forced discussions about inadequacies in their system into the US Congress.

But this has not happened to the same extent in Europe. One senior US official asked me why the European media has not scrutinised device regulation in the way that the American press had. In the States, Europe has been held up as an example of how bad things can actually get – with patients on this side of the Atlantic having been described as 'guinea pigs'.

A joint *BMJ*/Channel 4 *Dispatches* in May this year didn't do much to quell concerns. The EU system of approval by agreement between manufacturer and a commercial regulatory body operates under conditions of almost total commercial secrecy and is overseen in a hands-off manner by national regulatory authorities. Manufacturers submit data to a private body, which then assesses it to see if it is fit for market, and it is then allowed to display a CE mark. It is the same process that non-medical products such as mobile phones and toys go through.

As Nick Freemantle, professor of epidemiology at UCL, said: 'The current European regulatory framework – CE marking – might provide sufficient safeguards for electric toasters and kettles, but it is not adequate for treatments that can affect symptoms, health related quality of life, serious morbidity and mortality.'

Representatives of device manufacturers say that the European light touch regulation approach is fine – that there is no evidence it is any worse than America's. But, as the medical adage goes, absence of evidence is not evidence of absence.

There is no way of knowing what percentage of serious medical devices are faulty, poorly designed or have had to be recalled, because the European authorities have no centrally maintained register listing the devices on the market. In short, they do not know exactly what patients have had put into them in the first place.

Europe is an example of how bad things can actually get

Nor do they know on what evidence market entry was based. No European governmental regulator has it – scientific data sits with the manufacturers and the private companies that 'approve' the device. As the head of device regulation in the US, Dr Jeffrey Shuren, said: 'For the public in the EU, there is no transparency. The approval [requirements] are just what deal is cut between the device company and the private [organisation].'

Even data about devices that have been pulled from the market is virtually impossible to come by. When the *BMJ* – together with two doctors from Oxford University – contacted 192 manufacturers of withdrawn medical devices requesting evidence of the clinical data used to approve their devices, they denied us access, claiming that 'clinical data is proprietary information', that it was 'company confidential information', and that they could discuss only 'publicly available information' – of which there is very little.

Likewise, when we asked the relevant commercial regulatory bodies for the scientific rationale for approval of various devices that had been recalled, the results were stark. This information was classed as confidential because they were working as a client on behalf of the manufacturers – not the people who have them implanted in their bodies.

Even the Freedom of Information Act is of little help in obtaining information on any adverse events. The *BMJ*/Channel 4 *Dispatches* attempts to get access to adverse incident reports for specific implantables from the UK national regulator through the act were thwarted because it is overridden by medical device legislation. Article 15 of the EU Medical Devices Directive states: 'Member States shall ensure that all the parties involved in the application of this Directive are bound to observe confidentiality with regard to all information obtained in carrying out their tasks.'

Even the Association of British Healthcare Industries, a trade organisation of device manufacturers, agrees that the lack of transparency leads to misunderstanding and mistrust. 'Today it is very hard for anyone, even manufacturers and authorities, let alone citizens, to find out what products are approved to be on the market. We would like to see enhanced transparency and information to patients, citizens and all EU government authorities.'

So what does this mean? It means that doctors and patients are left to trust the companies to provide them with information about the benefits and harms of using their products. But with little scrutiny, oversight and transparency, there are no guarantees of this being a fair reflection of what their data – where they have it – actually says.

But there is a movement for change. As Krumholz says: 'I think one day people will look back and say now wait a minute. Half of the data were beyond public view and yet people were making decisions every day about these products? How did you let that happen? And I'm not sure how we let it happen.

'But I hope we'll enter an era where that will be over, and in fact there will be a great sharing of data, that we'll be able to have a public dialogue that's truly informed by the totality of evidence, and that we'll be able to make choices that are based on all of that evidence, knowing that there are no perfect drugs. That's always going to be a trade off. But we ought to be informed by all the evidence when we're making these decisions.' ❑

© Deborah Cohen
40(4): 59/72
DOI: 10.1177/0306422011427791
www.indexoncensorship.org

Deborah Cohen is investigations editor of the *BMJ*

HAYFESTIVALSWORLDWIDE.ORG

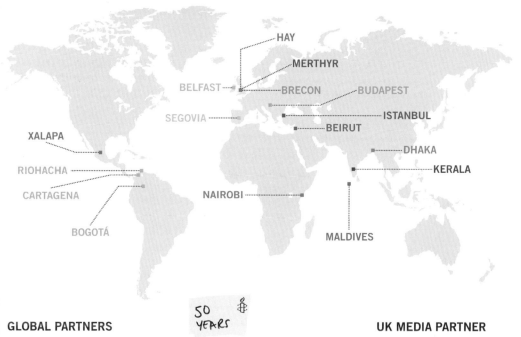

GLOBAL PARTNERS

50 YEARS

UK MEDIA PARTNER

BRITISH COUNCIL

AMNESTY INTERNATIONAL

Oxfam

The Telegraph

CARTAGENA
26–29 JAN 2012

MERTHYR
SEPT 2012

BEIRUT
MAY 2012

SEGOVIA
27–30 SEPT 2012

BUDAPEST
MARCH 2012

NAIROBI
14–16 SEPT 2012

BELFAST
JUNE 2012

ISTANBUL
OCT 2012

HAY
31 MAY–10 JUN 2012

MALDIVES
OCT 2012

XALAPA
OCT 2012

KERALA
NOV 2012

BRECON
AUG 2012

DHAKA
NOV 2012

For more than twenty years Hay Festival has brought writers, thinkers, musicians, film-makers and scientists together around the world to cross cultural and genre barriers and foster the exchange of ideas. Hay sets literature within a wider cultural and social context and creates high-definition live festivals and internationally resonant media impact. In Bill Clinton's famous phrase it is 'the Woodstock of the mind'.

Hay Festival is rooted in the Welsh book town of Hay-on-Wye. In 2009 we were awarded the Queen's Award for Enterprise: International Trade. There are now Hay Festivals in India, Bangladesh, Colombia, Kenya, Lebanon, Mexico and Spain as well as three in Wales.

The Woodstock of the Mind **BILL CLINTON**

In my mind it's replaced Christmas **TONY BENN**

THE QUEEN'S AWARDS FOR ENTERPRISE INTERNATIONAL TRADE

"One of the best festivals in the world" **THE INDEPENDENT**

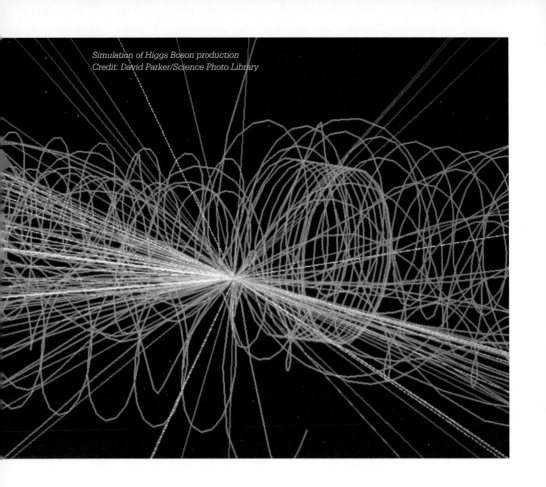

Simulation of Higgs Boson production
Credit: David Parker/Science Photo Library

DARING TO DOUBT

Science is full of uncertainty, so why the fear to express it? **Michael Blastland** reports

Earlier this summer, scientists thought they might have found the 'God particle', big news for physics, you can tell. Even so, the name is unfortunate and smacks too much of showbiz, for the God particle might not even exist.

Properly known as the Higgs Boson, this pip of a speck of a fragment of matter was postulated nearly 50 years ago to explain how other sub-atomic particles have mass. It popped into view, or seemed to, in a 27km circular tunnel under the French-Swiss border known as the Large Hadron Collider (LHC), dubbed the world's largest experiment.

Inside the LHC, proton particles are smashed together at fiendish speed while detectors examine short-lived traces of sub-atomic wreckage. The process sounds straightforward, though doubtless somewhat techie – at £6bn for the kit and running costs, it ought to be. So why did researchers say they only *thought* they *might* have found the Higgs Boson? Was it in the wreckage – or, more accurately, formed by the energy in the wreckage – or not?

Maybe. Not sure. Might be able to tell you later. Can you come back?

And that, believe it or not, is an underrated standpoint in science. The is-there/isn't-there saga of the Higgs Boson illustrates an important principle: that there's more uncertainty in science than science showbiz sometimes lets on.

There is also a compelling case to make this uncertainty explicit. They'd look prize lemons at the LHC if they announced that they'd found God, later to back down. Of which type of behaviour, more later – for, needless to say, not everyone sees the value in uncertainty this way. Disclosing it, like many forms of disclosure, is sometimes judged inconvenient or trivial.

The science ideal holds that all findings are provisional. Anyone can take away any result and try to replicate it. If it doesn't stand up, they can say so. But the issue here goes beyond arguing with people who have doubts about your results. It extends to proclaiming the uncertainty surrounding one's own results. It is about being first to point out the doubts, not the defensive last to acknowledge that yes, there might be something after all in other people's ifs and buts.

Why should anyone volunteer such humility? Because having done the research, they probably know already, or should do, where the doubts are. In part, this reassures us that enthusiasm for the answer is less likely to have run away with itself.

But since people may have invested any combination of heart, soul, years, energy, belief, money and reputation in their results, and since politics, employment and more money might depend on them, that's easier said than done. How would you feel about being invited to doubt your own research? A wholehearted, voluntary declaration of the uncertainties takes courage.

Is such an expectation naive? Let's first consider some reasons why uncertainty arises and then look at the case for talking more about it.

Imagine you are seeking to confirm the existence of the last tiger in the jungle. You find a rough outline of a footprint that looks promising. How can you be sure from this one footprint that there's really a tiger about? For you know that chance alone might from time to time produce a mark that looks tiger-like but isn't. To be more confident, you look for others, you seek confirmation. And until you have it, you remain cautious and uncertain. Proof in such a case is in large part statistical. How many footprints of what quality do we need before we believe?

Just so with the Higgs Boson – and also with another physics fragment lately in the news, the Wimp, or weakly interacting massive particle, sometimes known as dark matter. Researchers at the LHC found footprints resembling those that they expected for the Higgs Boson. But they did not find enough amid an immense quantity of data to be confident that this was the real thing. Was it, they wondered, merely an imposter shaped by chance debris?

So they announced their initial excitement but expressed caution, looked some more, only to be disappointed – still not enough footprints. Since then, they have begun to hunt the Higgs Boson in another part of the sub-atomic jungle. They're frank that it might not exist. They say they simply don't know.

A little further along the continuum of belief and evidence, Wimp hunters in Italy were reported recently to have found 67 hints of its existence from a quantity of experiments that suggested this was not likely to be the result of mere chance, but more likely to be evidence of the real thing. But they went no further. They did not announce a discovery, merely said that their results added to the weight of other evidence.

Mathematically-based science has a reputation for seeking certainty: hard facts nailed down with hard numbers. But statisticians, of all people, urge a modus operandi at odds with this reputation. Faced with uncertainty, they say, we must exercise caution – and by the way, there's oodles more uncertainty in nature's slow disclosure of its secrets than we might expect. An awful lot that appears meaningful at first sight turns out otherwise. There's nothing necessarily underhand in this. It is simply that in a big world chance sure gets around. Nature seems almost to play games with us, dangling meaning then snatching it away.

To one who cut his intellectual teeth in the humanities, it was a surprise to find that practitioners of a quantitative discipline went on about why their own findings might be wrong. Done properly, it is a mightily impressive act of self-discipline and rigour.

Those hunting the Higgs Boson similarly spoke of suggestive findings, not conclusive ones. They took pains to explain to journalists the risk of error brought about by chance resemblance. Don't get too excited, they said – though this was perhaps easier for them than others because they would be as curious if the Higgs Boson didn't exist as if it did. That is unusual. Negative findings – nothing doing – don't often set the pulse racing.

This type of uncertainty – the uncertainty arising from chance patterns and not-always-reliable hints – is one of many. There is also, for example, the structural uncertainty of modelling. That is, is your understanding of the way in which this event combined with that force leads to such-and-such an outcome as part of some natural process, and through which you hope to pump some numbers to see how they come out at the other end, a sufficiently accurate or useful representation of what really happens?

And we can't talk about uncertainty these days without also mentioning what is now known colloquially as Black Swan or Rumsfeldian uncertainty, the unknown unknowns that might bite you on the ankle with something you never thought of. Blindness to the possibility of Black Swans in finance, for all its quantitative sophistication, is often now said to have contributed to the 2008 banking crisis.

Negative findings don't often set the pulse racing

The analogy with the world of finance is useful. Banks and hedge funds rely on highly-paid mathematicians and economists – 'quants' – to evaluate risk. One quant I know of – more inclined to doubt than others – now teaches the numerati of the financial world to go to work each day applying what he calls devil's advocate risk management. Imagine, he says, that the bank has just lost $5bn. Now figure out how it happened, before it actually does. Since by definition it is not possible to know for sure about Black Swans in advance, the essence of this approach is to be restless for scenarios in which all that you fervently believe to be true, built as it may be on all manner of neat mathematics, is nevertheless wrong. Again, the humanities student is struck by how much quantification benefits from a good imagination for falsification.

These varieties of uncertainty need to be individually evaluated depending on the scientific research at issue. The uncertainty can even sometimes be roughly quantified. That is, it might be possible to say how likely you think you are to be wrong. So far, so responsible. And also all rather tedious, wouldn't you agree? Especially if you are worried about what other people will do with your admission of uncertainty – if you think they might use it, for example, as an excuse to ignore you.

And therein lies part of the danger. Caution in the face of uncertainty seldom makes news. It sounds plodding. In a sense, it *is* plodding. Doubt restrains, wearing a frown, suggesting (sometimes erroneously) inaction; confidence strides out with its teeth done. Uncertainty stands re-counting its fingers; assurance elbows the queue for headlines and a new grant. Bold claims, that's what tend to grab attention and win influence. Discoveries bright and hot. Breakthroughs. Shiny promises of new treatments, new technologies. Sunlit uplands of understanding. Or, on the other side, dire warnings and sudden dangers revealed.

In those cases where science also informs political decision-making, it's hardly a fair contest. The brassy assertion that the new dawn is within reach or a new threat imminent is an easy rhetorical win and might even, on occasion, be true. The hesitant confession of uncertainty is derided as ignorance, weakness or indecision. One only has to imagine the politician who stands before the electorate to say: 'Erm ...' No, the time for action is now, says the other side.

Let's take the dangerous example of climate science. Uncertainty in climate science can be affirmed without in any way implying a global hoax. To say that there are uncertainties here is to state the obvious and ought to be uncontroversial. But has the mainstream view on climate science suffered on occasion from a seeming desire to deny it?

In the controversy in 2009 now known as 'climategate', a server at the University of East Anglia (UEA) was hacked and emails emerged suggesting, among other things, reluctance to disclose data to critics, partly it seems for fear that they might mine it with a sceptical or mischievous eye for any uncertainty, or other evidence useful to their cause. (Several inquiries eventually exonerated UEA of any wrongdoing [see pp.113–119].)

A science writer at the *New York Times* commented at the time that some scientists were 'so focused on winning the public-relations war that they exaggerate their certitude – and ultimately undermine their own cause'.

There was also controversy the following year surrounding extravagant claims in a report by the Intergovernmental Panel on Climate Change (IPCC) about glacial melting. At about this time, *The Times* interviewed Sir John Beddington, the government's chief scientific adviser and a man with few doubts at all about the broad validity of mainstream climate science. The newspaper summarised his view thus: 'Public confidence in climate science would be improved if there were more openness about its uncertainties, even if that meant admitting that sceptics had been right on some hotly-disputed issues.'

He went on: 'I don't think it's healthy to dismiss proper scepticism. Science grows and improves in the light of criticism. There is a fundamental uncertainty about climate change prediction that can't be changed.'

The IPCC's claim that Himalayan glaciers would disappear by 2035 was, he reportedly said, part of a wider problem. 'Certain unqualified statements have been unfortunate. We have a problem in communicating uncertainty. There's definitely an issue there. If there wasn't, there wouldn't be the level of skepticism. All of these predictions have to be caveated by saying, "There's a level of uncertainty about that."'

So the question here is not only about the advisability of entering an argument. It's whether scientists censored the sophistication of their own understanding for the sake of a calculation about appearances. Not quite showbiz, but not far off. I suspect they probably knew – and still know – better than their opponents where the uncertainties are. Perhaps airing them feels like doing the devil's own work, perhaps there's fear of identifying potential weaknesses to attack. For science as public understanding, this is, I'd argue, ultimately anti-science. Acknowledging that there's uncertainty is not weakness but strength for at least two reasons: (a) it fosters trust; (b) it's usually true.

Seeking to resist the public recognition of uncertainty, if that's what happened, as if it would prove the proverbial nail in a shoe on which the whole battle could be lost, was ultimately bad strategy. No matter the short-term justification, it seems to have ended by exciting suspicion: 'What are you trying to hide?'

That argument applies regardless of the merits of the theory that climate change is a real result of human activity. You might be pleased at the damage done to that mainstream view; you might be appalled. That there has been damage seems hard to deny.

There seems to be a growing acceptance that all this could be handled better. In 2010, a review of the processes and procedures of the IPCC by the InterAcademy Council identified the communication of uncertainty as a key area for improvement.

Perhaps a more general problem is that there's too much shame in being honestly wrong, not enough in pretending to be right. Error has its uses; refusal to admit it or discuss its possible sources has none. In the league table of obstructive vanities, unwillingness in science to try to anticipate possible error or publicly explore the uncertainties ranks high.

That is, provided science and not politics is the game. In politics, winning on a false prospectus seems to be thought part of the rough and tumble, at least by some. So what if there were no weapons of mass destruction in Iraq? The principle justifying invasion remains correct, they might say, and if a dodgy dossier swayed a timid public, oh well. What's a doubt or two weighed against a greater cause? Science inevitably becomes embroiled in this from time to time. When it does, if it also becomes economical with the *actualité*, it's asking for trouble.

To all that, it might be said that hedging your bets only matters if your bets turn out badly. Why bother with this probabilistic fence-sitting if you're usually right in the end? So let's take another example where we might feel a personal interest in knowing that the standard answers are correct: medical research.

Is there too much readiness to discount the uncertainties?

Professor John Ioannidis, of Tufts University, is an authority on error in medical research. He finds plenty. I interviewed him a few years ago when few seemed to know quite how to respond to his arguments and evidence. One of his most cited papers, published in 2005, is called 'Why Most Published Research Findings Are False'. Ioannidis selected 49 of the most important research papers in medicine over 13 years – judging their importance by how often they were cited. Of these, 45 announced effective interventions. Thirty-four of these claims had been retested, and 14 of these, or 41 per cent, had been shown, he has said, 'to be wrong or significantly exaggerated'. He throws out aphorisms such as: 'The hotter a scientific field … the less likely the research findings are to be true.'

A few people don't like the way Ioannidis counts errors, but he would have to be very wrong indeed to be easily dismissed. At any rate, he poses uncomfortable questions. If so many findings turn out wrong in part or whole, what happens in the first place to the evidence that ought to exist to suggest that they were wrong? Are researchers too gung-ho in the hunt for a 'finding'? At the very least, is there too much readiness to discount the uncertainties?

To this suspicion that something is being lost we must also add the filtering effects of the media. For even when uncertainties are proclaimed loudly in their original academic publication, they tend to disappear when reported more widely. For example, if an academic paper offers a range of uncertainty around, for instance, a health risk, the media will typically seize on the figure at the most scary end of that range and say 'could be as high as …' The possibility at the lower end of the range vanishes. Some guidance in the media about whether a reported figure comes with reasonable hope of accuracy or is the kind that would struggle to hit a barn door would be useful. But that's not showbiz.

It has also been demonstrated in studies published in the *Lancet*, the *Journal of the American Medical Association* and elsewhere, and particularly in the work of Oxford University's Doug Altman – who first explained it to me – that there are malign filtering effects within the academic community. Altman makes the apparently undemanding argument that research ought to be reported fully and accurately, but offers much evidence that this does not happen, citing missing, incomplete or ambiguous information, in particular a lack of detail about methods and results, misleading interpretation and selective reporting.

Research claiming to have found something (positive) is more likely to be published than research that says it can find nothing either way (inconclusive) or that there is nothing to be found (negative). In fact, if you find nothing, you're less likely to bother offering it for publication in the first place. These effects are varieties of what's known as publication bias.

Publication bias is now a well known and largely accepted phenomenon – some journals are even trying to counteract it – but it has been only more recently explored than you might expect. Publication bias encourages research that claims to find a resounding 'yes' rather than a hesitant 'maybe'. The cumulative effect is to weed out many of the doubters.

One final example that involves media, politics and uncertainty: when Britain's medical authorities said in 2009 that there was a risk from swine flu that 65,000 people might die and one-third of the population become infected during the coming winter, they also said that the figure could be as low as 3,000 deaths – not at all unusual for the effects of your everyday humdrum winter flu.

As ranges of uncertainty go, that's pretty wide. This was barn-door territory. It was also the territory of frequent statements in Parliament, wall-to-wall news coverage, the stockpiling of medicines, school closures and plans to vaccinate everyone and the dog. Some public health specialists, however, were unhappy that the 65,000 figure ever saw the light of day. It was an extreme estimate, the result of taking the top-end estimate for the infection rate and combining that with the top-end estimate for the fatality rate. 'I would steer you well away from that 65,000 figure,' said the BBC's medical correspondent Fergus Walsh, in a rare media moment of anti-hype.

One for health officials in future might be to ask what would happen if they fessed up to the uncertainty: 'Honestly? We just don't know. Might be bad – and here's how bad if we really ramp up the worst-case scenarios, but we think that's a big outside bet. Might be nothing at all unusual for a winter. Seriously. Nothing much. Watch this space.' Whether that would imbue more panic or less is a moot point.

Thinking about how you'd bet on the possibilities is an idea advocated by David Spiegelhalter, professor of the public understanding of risk at Cambridge University. He also runs a website called Understanding Uncertainty (http://understandinguncertainty.org).

I should declare an interest. I know the professor and have been influenced by him. A newspaper comment piece he wrote last year was headlined: 'Scientists need the guts to say: I don't know.' He wrote: 'A popular view of scientists is that they deal with certainties, but they are (or should be) the first to admit the limitations in what they know.'

Mind you, there are also dangers in elevating respect for uncertainty. Junk or pseudo-science might attempt to clothe itself in the respectability of rational scepticism to attack a well-reasoned scientific consensus. Commercial interests have, on occasion, attempted to throw a vicious spanner in the works of scientific understanding and the public interest by suggesting that there are serious grounds for doubt and inaction even in the

Media coverage of the swine flu outbreak in the UK, 19 August 2009
Credit: Michael Kemp/Alamy

Evening Standard

NEWS EXTRA

SWINE FLU 'MASS GRAVES' PLAN

face of compelling evidence – of which perhaps the most notorious example is how smoking can damage your health.

And science is not always in the dark, of course. At some point, findings often become reliable. So some varieties of uncertainty might give way, eventually. But the sooner confronted, the sooner overcome. In what has come to be known as the 'Cargo Cult' address to the California Institute of Technology in 1974, the celebrated physicist Richard Feynman said: 'It's a kind of scientific integrity, a principle of scientific thought that corresponds to a kind of utter honesty – a kind of leaning over backwards. For example, if you're doing an experiment, you should report everything that you think might make it invalid – not only what you think is right about it … In summary, the idea is to try to give all of the information to help others to judge the value of your contribution – not just the information that leads to judgment in one particular direction or another.'

On holiday this year, I found myself among a group of hospital consultants and I asked how often they harboured serious doubts about whether the treatment they offered did any good. 'All the time,' they said. 'But sometimes people don't want to know about the uncertainties,' said one. 'They just want to be told they'll get better.' And sometimes such wishful thinking – via the placebo effect – works.

But I wouldn't want to rely on wishful thinking about positive results in science in general. I doubt the God particle believes in it. At least, in the spirit in which this article has been written, I think that's what I think. Naturally, I welcome your doubts. ❏

©Michael Blastland
40(4): 74/84
DOI: 10.1177/0306422011427623
www.indexoncensorship.org

Michael Blastland is a writer and broadcaster. His books include *The Tiger That Isn't* (Profile, co-writer Andrew Dilnot)

SAVING SOULS

Creationists have stepped up tactics and propaganda in the US to promote their cause. **Heather Weaver** assesses the damage

In 1925, the Tennessee Legislature passed the Butler Act, a law that prohibited public school employees from teaching 'any theory that denies the Story of the Divine Creation of man as taught in the Bible', including any theory 'that man has descended from a lower order of animals'. The statute led to the prosecution and conviction later that year of John T. Scopes, a high school biology teacher who dared to discuss evolution with his students. Scopes was represented by the American Civil Liberties Union (ACLU), a then relatively new organisation dedicated to preserving individual rights and liberties guaranteed by law. The proceedings – dubbed the 'Scopes Monkey Trial' by the media – attracted international attention, and the conviction was ultimately overturned. The Tennessee law was never enforced again and similar evolution bans across the country were, over a number of decades, defeated.

Eighty-six years later, the teaching of evolution is no longer a criminal act in any state. Indeed, though an organised movement of creationists has doggedly pursued various strategies to gain judicial approval for anti-evolution laws and other policies that seek to inject creationist beliefs into public school science curricula, American courts have repeatedly ruled that it is unlawful to censor the teaching of evolution in public schools or to use those schools to promote religious doctrine such as creationism. Despite its spectacular losses in the courts of law, however, the creationist movement marches on, and there is troubling evidence that it is growing increasingly successful in the court of public opinion, the political arena and public school classrooms.

Earlier this year, for example, the ACLU received a complaint from the parent of a fifth-grade student at an Alabama public school. His daughter's teacher had abruptly halted a science lesson after the topic of evolution had come up in the class textbook. The teacher announced that she would not read or discuss the issue further because 'some of us believe in God' and 'some of us believe that the world was made in seven days and that God created man and the trees'. When the ACLU pressed the school district regarding the incident, officials dismissed the teacher's actions as a 'stray comment' and claimed that they follow all state educational guidelines, which include teaching biological evolution. The ACLU continues to investigate the incident and is seeking documents that might help show whether, in fact, the school district's teachers are censoring evolution lessons in science classes. If so, however, they would scarcely be alone.

A study published in *Science* last January showed that only 28 per cent of US public high school biology teachers provide adequate instruction in evolution. According to the study, which was based on a national survey of public high school biology teachers, 13 per cent of teachers 'explicitly advocate creationism or intelligent design by spending at least one hour of class time presenting it in a positive light'. The remaining 60 per cent 'fail to explain the nature of scientific inquiry, undermine the authority of established experts, and legitimise creationist arguments'. As appears to be the case with the Alabama school teacher who refused to continue with her science lesson, many teachers within this failing 60 per cent no doubt intentionally undermine the teaching of evolution because they perceive it as conflicting with their personal religious views.

Many other teachers, however, merely want to avoid controversy and a backlash from students and parents, according to the study's authors, Penn State University political scientists Michael Berkman and Erik Plutzer. As Plutzer explained to Ars Technica, a science and technology news website: 'The challenge is for these teachers to stay out of trouble. They have to teach in a cautious way to avoid complaints from either side. They want to avoid what everyone wants to avoid, which is being called to the principal's office.'

With polls showing that more than two-thirds of Americans support teaching creationism in public schools – either as a replacement for or alongside evolution – it is not surprising that this caution has led to instruction that not only understates the scientific case for evolution but also gives credence to and endorses creationist religious beliefs.

Creationist leaders are well aware of their success on this front and will not ease the pressure on teachers any time soon. They blame the discoveries of modern science, especially evolution, for destroying traditional notions of both God and man, giving rise to moral relativism, and thereby causing a host of societal ills. For them, then, the fight against evolution is a central battle in the so-called culture wars; it is a fight to reclaim our humanity and save our souls by restoring America and Americans to God. With the stakes so high, creationists will thus continue to do whatever they must to suppress the teaching of evolution in public schools, no matter the cost; and in light of the courts' refusal to sustain outright attacks on evolution or permit teaching creationism alongside it, that means targeting teachers directly and indirectly.

Among other tactics employed in recent years, creationists have sponsored a barrage of proposed laws that would authorise teachers to introduce fabricated 'weaknesses' of evolution into individual science classes. They have also launched a high-profile anti-evolution propaganda campaign. These tactics aim to popularise creationist doctrine and anti-evolution beliefs. They ultimately seek to fashion a cultural environment that further emboldens willing teachers to flout the law by teaching creationism outright, while the remaining teachers are bullied into presenting students with incomplete and inaccurate information about evolution. Unfortunately, if the *Science* study is any indication, these tactics appear to be working.

To grasp just how insidious the creationist movement has become, it is helpful to understand its history. As Eugenie Scott and Nicholas Matzke of the National Center for Science Education chronicle in their 2007 paper, 'Biological Design in Science Classrooms', significant opposition to evolution education began in the 1920s 'as a byproduct of the acrimonious split of American Protestantism into "fundamentalist" and "modernist" camps'. While modernists treated the Bible as 'allegorical and a product of human history', fundamentalists adopted 'a strict doctrine of biblical inerrancy, wherein the entire text of the Bible was considered to be divinely inspired truth and without error (and usually, but not always, to be interpreted literally)'.

Fundamentalists' original focus on evolution education in the public schools makes even more sense for the contemporary creationist movement.

The John Scopes trial, Dayton, Tennessee, 17 July 1925
Credit: AP/Press Association

Thanks to mandatory attendance laws, the public schools offer access to a wide audience of students and families, including those of other faiths and non-believers. By targeting students in elementary and secondary school, creationists reach children when they are most impressionable and likely to internalise religious beliefs. By delivering religious doctrine through trusted teachers, they increase the likelihood that students will be less resistant to or questioning of religious doctrine, especially where, as is often the case today, the religious doctrine is cloaked in pseudo-science terms.

But the advantages of this approach are the very factors that have doomed it under the law. The First Amendment of the US Constitution contains the 'Establishment Clause', which prohibits the government from promoting or advancing religion. The US Supreme Court, the highest court in the country, has been particularly vigilant about enforcing this principle in public schools because of compulsory attendance laws, the vulnerability of children, and the special trust that families place in the government to educate their children with exploiting that opportunity to religiously indoctrinate them. As a result, the Supreme Court and lower courts have repeatedly rejected both efforts to incorporate instruction in creationism, creation-science, and intelligent design into public school curricula and efforts to undermine the teaching of evolution because of its perceived conflict with the Bible. After each judicial defeat, however, creationists have adapted their tactics and unrepentantly pressed forward, prompting many to comment on the irony of an evolving anti-evolution movement.

Though the Scopes Trial shone a light on the exploitation of the public schools to promote creationism and censor teaching about evolution, due to the fundamentalist movement and laws such as the Butler Act, evolution education in secondary public schools largely ground to a halt for several decades. It was not, as Scott and Matzke note, until the 50s and 60s – when fears arose that the country was falling behind the Soviet Union in technology and science – that evolution was reintroduced into many public school curricula via federally funded and commissioned textbooks written by scientists.

That effort was helped along by a 1968 Supreme Court decision overturning a state ban on teaching evolution in public schools. Susan Epperson, a tenth grade biology teacher at Little Rock Central High School, challenged the Arkansas law, which prohibited public school teachers from teaching, or using textbooks that teach, human evolution. Much to the dismay of fundamentalists, the Supreme Court agreed that the law was an unconstitutional 'attempt to blot out a particular theory because of its supposed conflict with the biblical account, literally read'.

The events of the 50s and 60s, as well as the Epperson ruling, prompted supporters of creationism to alter their approach. They next tried to dress up their religious belief as 'creation-science' and mandate that it be given 'equal time' alongside evolution in science classes. The Supreme Court once again rebuffed the attempt to suppress evolution teaching and promote creationism. In 1987, the Court struck down Louisiana's Balanced Treatment for Creation-Science and Evolution-Science in Public School Instruction Act. The law forbade the teaching of evolution in public schools unless accompanied by instruction in creation-science. The Court ruled that the 'state may not constitutionally prohibit the teaching of evolution in the public schools, for there can be no non-religious reason for such a prohibition'. Nor, the court added, could the state require 'the presentation of a religious viewpoint that rejects evolution in its entirety'.

Unable to banish evolution from public school classrooms and barred from using public schools to promote creationism, the creationist movement shifted course again, claiming to have developed a new scientific theory to rival evolution: so-called 'intelligent design', which posits that nature is so irreducibly complex that it must have been created by an 'intelligent designer'. In 1998, the Discovery Institute, a leading purveyor of intelligent-design creationism, produced a document detailing its plan to use intelligent design theory to drive a 'wedge' into the scientific community, combat the growing acceptance of evolution in America, and 'replace it with a science consonant with Christian and theistic convictions'. Key prongs of the wedge strategy included: (1) producing 'solid' scholarship, research and argument (2) formally integrating teaching about intelligent design into public school science standards and curricula and (3) popularising design theory among influential leaders, the media, and in the 'broader culture'.

The movement never came close to reaching the first goal: intelligent design proponents were unable to produce any credible scientific research to buttress their belief. In addition, the campaign to formally incorporate intelligent design into public school curricula as a legitimate alternative to evolution also failed after a federal judge ruled in 2006 that intelligent design is just another extension of creationism, there is no scientific evidence to support it, and it cannot be taught in public schools.

The case *Kitzmiller v Dover Area School District* was brought by the ACLU, Americans United for Separation of Church and State and the law firm Pepper Hamilton on behalf of parents and students who objected to a District policy that aimed to make students 'aware of gaps/problems in Darwin's theory and of other theories of evolution including, but not limited to, intelligent design'. The policy required science teachers to instruct all ninth-grade biology students that evolution is a theory and 'not a fact', that '[g]aps in the Theory exist for which there is no evidence' and that '[i]ntelligent Design is an explanation of the origin of life that differs from Darwin's view'.

During a six-week trial in the case, federal district court Judge John Jones, an appointee of then-president George W. Bush, heard testimony from experts regarding the nature of evolution and intelligent design. Like the Scopes Trial, the Dover proceedings attracted national and international attention and was widely seen as a test of the influence that the modern creationist movement – now more sophisticated, better organised and well funded – could wield in the legal arena.

Plaintiffs' lawyers argued that intelligent design is a religious belief that simply does not meet the rigorous requirements of science and thus should not be presented alongside evolution in public school science

Intelligent design v Darwin, Dover, Pennsylvania, December 2005
Credit: Sipa/Rex Features

classes. In the end, the court agreed, sharply rebuking the claim that intelligent design is a valid scientific theory. In a sweeping review of the evidence, the court ruled that science is 'limited to empirical, observable and ultimately testable data', while intelligent design (like its predecessor, creation-science) 'is reliant upon forces acting outside of the natural world, forces that we cannot see, replicate, control or test, which have produced changes in this world'. The court concluded that, although 'Darwin's theory of evolution is imperfect … the fact that a scientific theory cannot yet render an explanation on every point should not be used as a pretext to thrust an untestable alternative hypothesis grounded in religion into the science classroom or to misrepresent well-established scientific propositions'.

Despite these failures, the wedge strategy was successful in one key respect – thrusting evolution and creationism back in the spotlight in a way that had not been achieved since the Scopes Trial. The Dover trial placed evolution at the center of the culture wars, popularising intelligent design and gaining prominent, vocal political support for teaching it in public schools. At the height of the coverage and controversy, Discovery Institute operatives and other creationists pressed their message everywhere they could, including in newspapers and other print media, television, and radio. This expansive exposure was an enormous boost to the creationist movement, and it set the stage for future propaganda campaigns. It also led then-president George W Bush to endorse the teaching of intelligent design in public schools, lending more credibility to the movement. Bush, who had previously stated that the jury is still out on evolution, declared during a 2005 press conference that '[b]oth sides ought to be properly taught ... so people can understand what the debate is about'.

After the court's ruling in Dover, creationism advocates were again forced to adapt their legal strategies. Their hopes of formally incorporating creationism, via intelligent design theory, into public school curricula dashed, they turned to subtler, more indirect ways to undermine evolution education. Drawing on intelligent design theory's argument that evolution contains 'gaps' in information, they have increasingly focused on the claim that there is controversy in the scientific community regarding the purported 'strengths and weaknesses' of evolutionary theory. They attack those who oppose incorporating this alleged controversy into science curricula as trampling free speech and seeking to brainwash students against critical analysis of scientific matters.

Specifically, under the pretexts of protecting the academic freedom of those who question evolution and fostering students' critical thinking skills, creationism advocates have been instrumental in proposing a number of state laws that would encourage and authorise public school teachers to present the so-called 'weaknesses' of evolution and other purportedly controversial scientific theories, such as global warming. More than 40 bills of this type have been proposed in 13 states over the past seven years. Creationists have also sought to inject the 'weaknesses' argument into state science educational standards, which govern public school science curricula and textbook approval processes.

The invocation of 'academic freedom' and 'critical analysis' to defend and advance a campaign singularly aimed at censoring proven scientific principles and promoting, in their stead, untested and unverifiable religious ideology would be laughable if it weren't for the serious risk that these tactics pose to sound science education. As Judge Jones so artfully laid out in the Dover case, there is, of course, no controversy in the scientific community about the soundness of evolution as a scientific principle any more than there is a dispute over the validity of the theory of gravity. The purported 'weaknesses' that sponsors of these measures hope will be presented to students are recycled claims – universally rejected by scientists – that have been made for years by creationism and intelligent design advocates. There is no academic freedom in the right to provide demonstrably false information to students, and ensuring that information presented in science classes meets basic, well-established scientific standards enhances students' ability to engage in critical analysis.

Workshops declare that evolution is 'bad science'

Fortunately, due to strenuous opposition by the ACLU and other groups, nearly all of these legislative efforts have, thus far, been defeated. (Louisiana remains the only state to have passed an 'academic freedom' bill – the Louisiana Science Education Act.) But the campaign of misinformation has nevertheless been remarkably effective in confusing the public about the scientific support for evolution. While 57 per cent of Americans believe that humans and other living things have evolved over time, according to a poll conducted this September by the Public Religion Research Institute, only half (51 per cent) of those polled knew that there is also a broad scientific consensus supporting evolution. Over a quarter of respondents erroneously believed that scientists are divided on the question, and a mind-boggling 15 per cent of those polled thought that most scientists do not endorse evolution as a valid scientific principle. Seizing on this confusion, creationists have, in recent years, ramped up their propaganda efforts to gain and solidify public support for their cause.

As the modern creationist movement has become more organised and gained more exposure, it has also become better financed, allowing for grander and wider-reaching propaganda efforts. Answers in Genesis (AIG) and the Discovery Institute, two leading creationist groups, in particular, have successfully marshalled resources to mount multi-million-dollar projects intended to bring the public into the anti-evolution fold. In 2007, AIG, a young-earth creationist group that believes the earth and humans were created only 6,000 years ago, opened the Creation Museum in Kentucky. The state-of-the-art 70,000 square foot museum reportedly was funded with more than $25m in donations. It was conceived as a destination attraction, and features a number of exhibits that promote the biblical account of creationism and creation-science and deny the validity of evolution. Workshops offered by the museum, for example, declare that evolution is 'bad science'. Exhibits explain that while 'dinosaurs were created on the same day as humans and lived with us', most 'were destroyed in the worldwide Flood that God sent to judge the earth, but two of each kind survived to inspire the dragon legends that permeate most cultures of the world'. By 2010, AIG claimed that over one million people had visited the museum and, based on its success, it is now planning to build (taking advantage of millions of dollars in tax breaks) a Noah's Ark theme park elsewhere in Kentucky. The Ark Park will likely echo the themes of the Creation Museum when it comes to evolution.

In another high-profile propaganda campaign, creationists managed several years ago to produce and distribute a major motion picture documentary, *Expelled: No Intelligence Allowed*. The film, which cost over $3m to make, was released nationally and purported to uncover a broad conspiracy in the scientific community to ignore evidence contradicting evolution and silence those trying to bring to light the evidence. The film's rampant misinformation and outright lies are well-documented by the National Center for Science Education at its special website 'Expelled Exposed'. In the film, host Ben Stein, an actor and former speechwriter for Richard Nixon, also claims that Darwin and evolution supporters are to blame for eugenics, Nazism and the Holocaust. The fact that producers chose Stein to narrate and host a film that claims to stand against the persecution of good teachers is, in itself, ironic and an affront to actual schoolteachers: Stein's main claim to fame is his small role playing one of the worst teachers ever depicted on film in *Ferris Bueller's Day Off*. (In the realm of 'celebrity' spokespeople for the creationist movement, Stein is the top dog – though former television star Kirk Cameron, who starred in the 80s sitcom *Growing Pains*, might be poised to overtake him. Cameron has spoken widely against evolution education and even created and marketed his own board game, 'Intelligent Design vs. Evolution'.) The film labels scientists who recognise the validity of evolution as Nazis, revealing its true nature as a piece of anti-science propaganda.

If creationists' early strikes against evolution education were, based on their direct and obvious attack strategies, akin to conventional warfare, their latest tactics are more analogous to those of guerilla fighters. After trying for decades, with little success, to enact formal legal change that would censor the teaching of evolution and instead permit creationist beliefs to be advanced in public schools, creationists appear to be embracing another approach that targets teachers more indirectly. By spreading misinformation and propaganda about evolution and inflaming the public debate over it, they have managed to create a cultural environment in which some teachers feel inspired to violate the law on their own by teaching creation, and many others – cognisant of the potential backlash from parents and students who might otherwise, however wrongly, perceive the teachers as challenging or denigrating their religious beliefs by endorsing evolution as a proven scientific concept – feel pressured to self-censor their science lessons.

Even the current legal strategies (relating to evolution's so-called 'strengths and weaknesses') avoid any direct attacks on evolution or direct advocacy of creationism or intelligent design. Instead, creationists now seek to exploit teachers' instincts to avoid controversy by giving them legal cover to present information that will placate those who dispute evolution on religious grounds.

The fallout from this decades-long campaign to dismantle evolution education and re-insert religious ideology into public school science classes is substantial and disturbing. Nearly three-quarters of students are receiving an inadequate foundation in science education. As creationists ratchet up and hone their current strategies targeted at teachers, these figures may grow worse. Consequently, millions of students are and will continue to be ill-prepared for the rigours of higher education and less likely to pursue careers in scientific fields. Much like the mid-20th century, when we discovered that the country was falling behind the world in technology and science, the US continues to lag far behind other nations in science education: a 2009 study by the Organisation for Economic Co-operation and Development rated US science students in the bottom ten of the top 30 industrialised nations.

Creationists' treatment of evolution as opinion, rather than scientific fact, is also likely to encourage devaluing scientific discovery in other contexts as well. Indeed, global warming deniers have already hitched their wagons to the evolution 'debate' by casting global warming as another 'scientific controversy' about which science curricula should remain circumspect.

In addition to the serious harm caused to science education, the use of public schools to advance religious ideology infringes the constitutional rights of every student to be free from government-imposed religious indoctrination. It also usurps the rights of parents, not the government, to control the religious upbringing of their children. And it creates religious dissension that undermines a core function of the public school system, which, as one Supreme Court justice has observed, was '[d]esigned to serve as perhaps the most powerful agency for promoting cohesion among a heterogeneous democratic people' and must, therefore, be kept 'scrupulously free from entanglement in the strife of [religious] sects'.

Though the courts and legislatures have traditionally marked the front-line for combatting the creationist movement, the battlelines are shifting. Make no mistake, it remains important to defend those judicial victories and to ensure that no ground is yielded in the legal sphere. But to truly protect science education in US public schools, we also must look beyond the courts and devise strategies to ease the pressure on science teachers to self-censor or otherwise compromise their instruction in evolution – starting with a plan to open the public's eyes to the overwhelming evidence and support for evolution in the scientific community, the primacy of evolution as a fundamental principle of biology and science, and the importance of sound science to our individual and common welfare. ❏

©Heather Weaver
40(4): 87/98
DOI: 10.1177/0306422011428559
www.indexoncensorship.org

Heather Weaver is staff attorney for the ACLU Program on Freedom of Religion

Optimise the release of energy from our diet

Sleep on the left to avoid stillbirth

modulates the harmful effects of electromagnetic radiation

Olive oil cuts risk of stroke by 41%

GM trial vandalised

benefits of wheatgrass juice

clinically proven to rebuild stem cells

head massage in schools

'MRSA-resistant' pyjamas

shun the obscure chemicals

Can goats' blood help beat MS?

Scientist silenced by libel threat

Sense About Science is a charity that helps people to make sense of science and evidence. We stand up for scientific debate, free from stigma, intimidation, hysteria or censorship.

And we encourage everyone, whatever their experience, to insist on evidence in public life.

Current programmes include:

- **Ask For Evidence**: our campaign to get people asking advertisers, government bodies, companies, and other organisations to set out evidence for the claims they make.

- **Seeking reform of the libel laws**: protecting open scientific discussion.

- **Responding to misinformation**: working with scientists to tackle dodgy science claims and stop the spread of misinformation on subjects from extreme weather to miracle cures.

- **Making sense of uncertainty on scientific and medical issues**: helping people to establish what is known and how.

People are damaged and disempowered by misleading claims, whether on advertising material, campaign statements or policy announcements. Understanding evidence is important to a rational, fairer, more accountable society.

Support us: Donate, campaign and lend your support at
www.senseaboutscience.org or **www.justgiving.com/senseaboutscience**,
or email **enquiries@senseaboutscience.org**.
Follow us: @senseaboutsci #askforevidence.

senseaboutscience.org

sense about science

BURDEN OF PROOF

Science is the ultimate totalitarian regime, says **Michael Brooks**. Could it work any other way?

If he worked in any other sphere, marine biologist Donald Williamson might get a bit of sympathy – maybe even kindness. In 1990, he slipped and fell while collecting samples on a beach. Ever since, he has been confined to a wheelchair. The accident didn't stop him contributing to science, even in his late 80s. But to his scientist colleagues, this human tragedy means nothing: his ideas are still 'the most stupid thing that has ever been proposed'.

In August 2009, Williamson published a paper on the origin of butterflies. Once upon a time, he suggested, a winged insect inadvertently fertilised its eggs with sperm from a velvet worm. It's easy to see what Williamson was thinking. Male velvet worms place their sperm on the female's skin, rather than anywhere out of sight, so an insect could pick it up. What's more, these worms do look a bit like the larvae of Micropterix, a relative of the butterflies. If the hybridisation did happen, the Earth might have seen the birth of an organism girded with two separate body growth programmes in its DNA: one larval, one for a winged insect. Hey presto: the mysterious double-life cycle of the butterfly.

The idea passed enough muster to be published in the *Proceedings of the US National Academy of Sciences*. And then the knives came out. While lay observers might consider it an interesting and worthwhile contribution, most scientists working in insect development were ruthless. One said the paper would be more suited to the '*National Enquirer* than the National Academy'. Another was less emotive but similarly dismissive: 'The paper is hypothetical and speculative and not a single bit of evidence supports the idea.'

Williamson, who will be 90 in January, has said he is 'on a straight-line course for posthumous recognition'. His peers disagree: there will be no recognition, posthumous or otherwise, because his contention is 'bizarre and unsupported'. Examination of the genomes of the creatures involved show no evidence in the idea's favour, and Williamson's 'execrable piece of work' has been torn to shreds.

Science is brutal. The physicist Carl Sagan once wrote that its pursuit creates 'a roiling sea of jealousies, ambition, backbiting, suppression of dissent, and absurd conceits'. It is a totalitarian regime living among us. But this, it can be argued, is a strength, not a weakness.

Though it seems harsh and heartless at times, science owes its success to the hard time that new ideas receive. They must pass the test of experiment, then verification of that experiment, and even then a scientist's peers and colleagues will call for extraordinary evidence if the results fly in the face of accepted wisdom. When Italian researchers suggested they had seen neutrinos flying at faster-than-light speeds in September this year, excited news stories abounded, but scientists showed nothing but intense scepticism. Why? According to Einstein's special theory of relativity, nothing can travel faster than light. Reports of a break in the law of physics might provoke journalists to dizzy speculation, but scientists are much harder to move: extraordinary claims, as the adage goes, require extraordinary evidence.

Even when extraordinary evidence is in hand, recognition is not guaranteed; some ideas wait in the wings for decades before achieving the status of orthodoxy. Those who came up with the idea might be long dead by then. Alfred Wegener, who first proposed that the continents might have drifted across the surface of the earth, had been dead 34 years before his notion was accepted.

Science, then, lives on the horns of a dilemma. In order to progress, it must destroy its most cherished truths. And it does that only when it absolutely must.

Nature abhors a vacuum but not as much as scientists

The philosopher of science Thomas Kuhn addressed this issue in his 1962 book *The Structure of Scientific Revolutions*. Citing example after example, Kuhn showed that our understanding of the universe progresses through a gradual process of evidence piling up against an orthodoxy until it can no longer be ignored. This is the moment Kuhn called 'crisis'. The trouble is, it is not enough for an orthodoxy to fail all experimental tests; there must be a replacement that can be slotted into the failing paradigm's place. Nature abhors a vacuum, but not as much as scientists do.

That is why Ptolemy's theory describing the way the planets orbited Earth had to be tweaked every time problematic new data came in. Until Copernicus arrived with the extraordinary and heretical (to scientists as well as the Church) notion that Earth and the other planets orbit the sun, there was no alternative but to add new 'epicycles' to the Ptolemaic system.

A contemporary example is the scientific explanation for how we distinguish between scents. We know that the nose contains variously-shaped pockets, known as receptors, into which odiferous molecules lodge. Some molecules 'turn on' the receptors, causing them to send an electrical signal into the brain.

The standard view is that it is a 'lock and key' mechanism: only if the molecule has the right shape to unlock the receptor will the signal be sent. It sounds plausible, but we can recognise around 100,000 smells, and have only 400 differently-shaped smell receptors. More problematic still, some chemicals smell similar but look very different, while others have the same shape but smell different.

There is a competing theory that is a much better fit – it has to do with the way the molecules vibrate. However, it has almost no traction within the smell-researching community because, for now, shape simply remains the dominant paradigm, and crisis point has not yet been reached.

Trace this desire to stick with the orthodoxy down to its source and we find that the problem is human beings. The astronomer Donald Fernie once made a wry observation about the tribal instincts of those working in his field: 'There are times when we resemble nothing so much as a herd of antelope, heads down in tight formation, thundering with firm determination in a particular direction across the plain', he said. 'At a given signal from the leader we whirl about, and, with equally firm determination, thunder off in a quite different direction, still in tight parallel formation.'

Fernie's invocation of the leader's role is telling. Science is meant to be about ideas, laws and principles, rather than the inclinations of a senior figure. But science is a human endeavour, and humans have always followed leaders. Here's what biologist Carl Lindegren had to say on the subject:

> One likes to think of science as divorced from personalities because one seeks the guidance of a principle rather than a person. Thus, the individual scientist experiences a feeling of freedom since he has the impression he lives in a community in which the law and not the man is the ultimate arbiter. This truly democratic practice has led to the fallaciously democratic practice of determining the validity of a scientific view by finding out how many other scientists agree with it. Voting in this context is so much influenced by past training and indoctrination that it tends to reject the new and to reaffirm the old.

This has repercussions in funding, of course: the money is distributed on the recommendations of senior figures, most of whom have a vested inter-est in ensuring future research validates the orthodoxy they helped establish.

If further proof were required that science runs along totalitarian lines, it is the fact that acts of sedition and anarchy are the only way to make progress.

Faced with overwhelming scepticism from the medical establishment, Australian doctor Barry Marshall resorted to self-experiment in order to prove that bacteria are the most common cause of stomach ulcers. In an experiment carried out without ethical approval, and with the risk of serious danger to his own health, Marshall drank a cupful of the bacteria he believed caused ulcers. The ensuing illness and the results of biopsies of Marshall's stomach (carried out by colleagues who took a 'don't ask, don't tell' attitude) forced a complete turnaround in the medical establishment's advice on stomach ulcers within just a few years. What had once been caused by stress, alcohol, smoking and poor diet was now, thanks to an underhand strike against the establishment, attributed to a pathogen.

There are many such stories in the history of medicine, but self-experiment without ethical approval is only one kind of anarchy. We learned the structure of DNA through similarly subversive means. Crick and Watson had been instructed to stop their research by bosses at Cambridge; they ignored the orders and carried on using methods that included what Crick referred to as 'burglary' of data from collaborators working at King's College London. No one knew how to copy DNA quickly until Kary Mullis established a different way of thinking about the problem by using psychoactive drugs, including LSD, to retrain his brain. He won a Nobel Prize for his troubles.

In the absence of strong supporting evidence, Stanley Prusiner shattered the paradigm of disease transmission by a programme of vigorous PR work on behalf of his 'prion hypothesis'. This was the idea that the transmission of diseases such as BSE and CJD involved a particle that Prusiner named a 'prion' – even though he couldn't define what a prion actually was. Colleagues howled (and some resigned) at his subversion of the normal scientific way of working: 'There's no point creating a name for something that we don't even know exists yet', one colleague complained. Nonetheless, Prusiner was rewarded with a Nobel Prize and a position of pre-eminence in the field – and he broke a long-standing deadlock in the pursuit of an understanding of these diseases.

Having been denied the chance to publish through normal channels, Lynn Margulis resorted to publishing a book on her hypothesis about how complex life emerged in evolutionary history. She 'didn't follow the rules and pissed a lot of people off', is how one expert put it.

Peuerbach planetary model by Erasmus Oswald Schreckenfuchs, an attempt to reconcile theories of Aristotle and Ptolemy, 1556
Credit: Royal Astronomical Society/Science Photo Library

Sphæra octaua & nona cum primo mobili, folio 390

In the light of such stories of rule-breaking in the pursuit of discovery, it is tempting to declare we should accelerate scientific progress by making it easier to challenge the orthodoxy. Perhaps, for instance, we should lower the standards required for a theory to be taken seriously, or for experimental proof to be accepted?

Though tempting, it is a fool's errand because nature is the only arbiter of science. As Galileo put it, 'Nature is inexorable and immutable; she never transgresses the laws imposed upon her, or cares a whit whether her abstruse reasons and methods of operation are understandable to men.' That is why scientists place such great store by the experiment. You can make up ideas about the way things are, but ask a question of nature, and she will soon set any delusions straight.

Modern science was founded with this attitude: the Royal Society's motto is *nullis in verbia*: take nobody's word for it. Scientific truth is established only through experiments carried out in the presence of, or communicated to, many witnesses who all agree on what has been observed and what it means.

That explains – partially, at least – why science progresses so slowly. Nature does not relinquish her secrets easily: experiments are difficult, and successful experiments are rare. Even rarer is the profound result whose implications are universally accepted. 'Nearly all scientific research leads nowhere,' Nobel laureate Sir Peter Medawar once said.

The difficulty of getting answers from nature is illustrated by the fact that scientists are already stretching the rules to breaking point.

In 2005, the journal *Nature* published a study entitled 'Scientists Behaving Badly'. It was based on a survey in which one-third of the scientists polled admitted to indulging in some kind of research misconduct in the previous three years. That might be anything from cherry-picking data that supported a favourite hypothesis to carrying out medical research without ethical approval.

Usually, the motivation is that, without bending the rules, generating reliable, reproducible results whose implications can be clearly drawn is just too hard. Another survey, published in 2006, said such rule-bending is 'normal misbehaviour' and plays 'a useful and irreplaceable role' in science.

To argue that scientists simply do experiments and accumulate a heap of indisputable facts is to miss the subtleties of the endeavour. 'Facts' are interpretations of the results of experiments. Those interpretations are not always correct, as Francis Crick and James Watson learned – almost to their cost. As they were racing towards a structure for DNA, the shadow of Linus

James Watson and Francis Crick with their model of part of a
DNA molecule, Cambridge, UK, 1953
Credit: A Barrington Brown/Science Photo Library

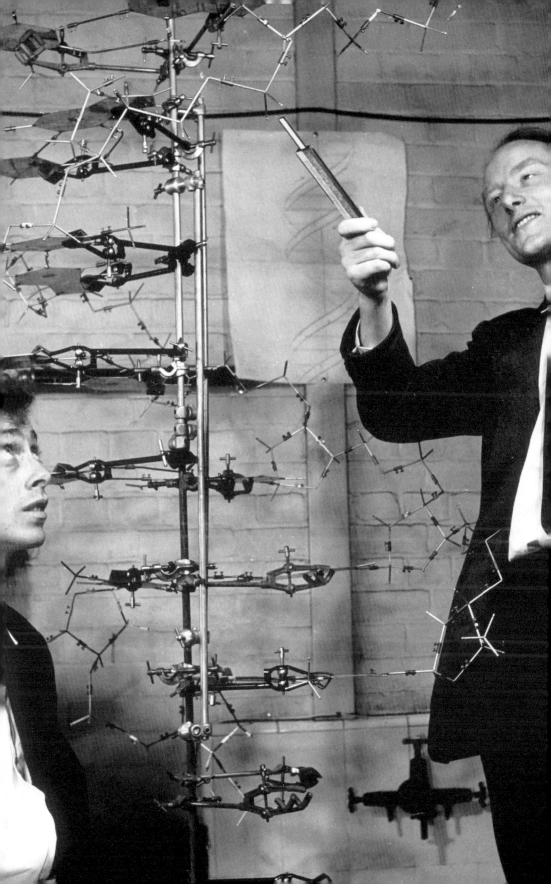

Pauling loomed large. Across the Atlantic, Pauling, an eminent chemist whose reputation eclipsed that of Crick and Watson, was also closing in on the answer. In order to get there first, Crick and Watson ditched an orthodoxy, in the form of the accepted value for the angle formed by a chemical bond. A colleague looking over their shoulder told them the textbook value was a guess that had been repeated so often it had gained the status of fact.

Crick said afterwards he learned 'not to place too much reliance on any single piece of experimental evidence'. Watson's view was similar: 'Some data was bound to be misleading if not plain wrong', he said.

Einstein was similarly unwilling to be a slave to experimental results. His theory of special relativity did not fit with data on the way electric and magnetic fields deflected beams of charged particles. A rival theory was far more 'accurate', but Einstein shrugged; he knew his theory was right, and the others wrong for other reasons. In the end, his scepticism about the accuracy of the data was proved right.

We can't, then, lower the bar on the practice of science; it has already been lowered as far as is commensurate with the reliability required of experiments.

There is another option, however. We can't make it easier to overthrow a regime, but we can shift the balance of power by increasing the number of revolutionaries on the attack, and reducing the numbers working in defence of the orthodoxy.

Scientists rely on a subsection of their population being possessed of the ego and tenacity of the adventurer seeking new mountains to climb and new territories to claim. These subversive, anarchic individuals are willing to question the orthodoxy and propose alternatives. The size of, and attitude towards, this minority group determines whether a particular field will thrive or stall.

At the moment, science does not attract these types in large numbers. The few studies that exist in this area suggest that students with extrovert characters drop mathematics and science subjects at the first opportunity. The most explicit study was done on Dutch schoolchildren, and published in 2010. Amongst the nearly 4,000 children studied, the researchers 'observed that students who took advanced mathematics, chemistry, and physics were less extroverted and more conscientious than students who chose a less science-oriented set of subjects'.

Clearly, students' subject choices are related to their personality. If science wants to help itself battle orthodoxy, and thus make better progress, it has to address its lack of appeal to risk-taking, adventurous types.

There is just one problem with this: the rewards are extremely hard to quantify. Scientists rarely get rich. Even fewer of them become famous. The French physiologist Claude Bernard called the joy of discovery 'the liveliest that the mind of man can ever feel', but it's hard to sell that joy to a generation that has never experienced it. Then there is the appalling treatment meted out to many dissenters, the likelihood that the dissent is misguided anyway, and the possibility of limited or no recognition within your lifetime even if you are right.

Battling the totalitarianism of science is not for the faint-hearted or the thin-skinned, so who would choose the role of the scientific revolutionary? The answer comes from the man who won a Nobel prize for his discovery of vitamin C. 'Research uses real egotists who seek their own pleasure and satisfaction, but find it in solving the puzzles of nature', said Albert Szent-Györgyi.

Great science is done by those driven so hard by a selfish desire to pry open nature's secrets that they are willing to risk the oppression and condemnation of their colleagues. Such characters are few and far between; rather than worry about suppression of dissent, we should perhaps be grateful that 400 years of science has produced enough of these people to get us where we are today. ❏

©Michael Brooks
40(4): 100/109
DOI: 10.1177/0306422011427654
www.indexoncensorship.org

Michael Brooks is an author, journalist and broadcaster. He has a PhD in quantum physics and is a consultant for *New Scientist*. His most recent book is *Free Radicals* (Profile)

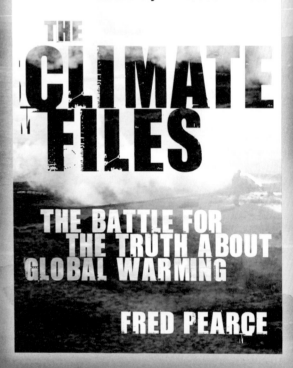

INFORMATION GAP

Scientists were the first to use the internet to share their data. So why not let us all join in? **Fred Pearce** makes the argument for open access

Steve McIntyre is a pernickety Canadian. A retired mining geologist, trained mathematician and amateur climatologist, he has for the past eight years locked horns with the Climatic Research Unit (CRU) at the University of East Anglia, trying to gain access to their data on the history of global temperatures.

He is not (repeat: not) paid by, beholden to or in regular contact with fossil fuel companies or lobby groups trying to undermine climate change science. He is not even a climate sceptic. For years, McIntyre has been asking for CRU's 'crown jewels', raw data assembled from weather stations round the world that it says proves how much the world has warmed in the past 160 years.

He does not believe this conclusion is a big lie. But he does want to see for himself. And in particular to look at how the data had been 'manipulated' – a perfectly honourable process in which, for instance, some weather stations are made to count for more than others because they represent large areas with few weather stations, while others are discounted because their rural locations have been invaded by growing cities.

It's not what everybody wants to do on a Saturday night, but surely he is exactly the kind of citizen investigator the 2000 Freedom of Information Act was intended to help.

Of course, his persistence has not made him a friend of CRU's director Phil Jones. The crown jewels are his life's work. For years Jones held out, with the backing of his university's Freedom of Information (FOI) officers, from releasing the data to McIntyre. Jones said it was commercially valuable. He said it was his intellectual property. He said revealing it would damage international relations. CRU has been congenitally hostile to FOI requests from McIntyre and others. At the end of 2009, 105 FOI requests had been submitted to UEA for CRU data, of which only ten had been acceded to in full.

The battle between the two men for the crown jewels was the backdrop – and very possibly the motive – for the still-mysterious hacking of CRU's emails and their publication online at the end of 2009. Much of the world's science community sided with Jones in the resulting 'climategate' saga, condemning what they regarded as politically and commercially motivated attacks on their research.

But others took McIntyre's side, seeing him as a data libertarian. And last June, following a new request for the data from Jonathan Jones, an Oxford physicist and 'climate agnostic', the FOI's commissioner, Christopher Graham, finally ruled that the crown jewels should be handed over. And they were, a month later. The world did not fall in.

If CRU had been more open with its data from the start, a great deal of time and angst on the part of its scientists – and a great deal of public uttering of paranoid nonsense from climate deniers – would have been avoided. And if, in the months before the hack, Jones and his colleagues had not spent ever more time bitching about McIntyre and scheming to keep their data and working methods secret, then the emails would have contained little of outside interest.

Graham's decision unlocks some four million temperature readings taken at 4,000 weather stations over the past 160 years. But as the journalist Jonathan Jones put it, 'the most significant features of this decision are the precedents that have been set'. It could open the door to thousands of other British researchers being required to share their data with the public. Good.

Under the 2000 Freedom of Information Act, universities, like other public institutions, must share their data unless there are good reasons not to. It is now clear that the good reasons have to be just that – not excuses. Graham, who is the final arbiter in FOI requests, was scathing in his ruling that CRU claims that sharing data would harm international relations were

Professor Phil Jones, Director of the Climatic Research Unit, appears before the Science and Technology Committee in Portcullis House, London, 1 March 2010
Credit: PA

'highly speculative'. And on commercial considerations, he noted acidly: 'it is not clear how UEA might have planned to commercially exploit the information'.

But should all publicly funded data be free, and all publicly funded researchers required to hand it over? In an age when data distribution is so easy, it is hard to make a case that sharing data is just too hard. After the military, scientific researchers were the first people to use the internet, precisely so they could share large data sets among themselves. So why not let us all join in? But what about emails and research notes and the data from failed experiments? Some believe requests for such stuff would both damage research and overwhelm researchers. And some think your access should depend on who you are.

At the same time as the climategate FOI requests began building up at CRU, the giant tobacco company Philip Morris began – initially anonymously

– asking for data from Scottish researchers who had interviewed thousands of teenage smokers on what they thought about tobacco marketing. Not only was this expensive research – paid for by a cancer charity – it was also, as the head of the Stirling University research unit Gerard Hastings put it, 'the sort of research that would get a tobacco company into trouble if it did it itself'.

The researchers have held out – and went public with their disgust in the *Independent* in September. But here's the bottom line. FOI legislation is 'applicant blind', as Maurice Frankel of the UK Campaign for Freedom of Information puts it. It does not matter if the thoughts of smoking teenagers are of interest to Philip Morris or the National Heart Foundation or someone who wants to stop their child from starting to smoke. They are, and should be, all the same. Otherwise Friends of the Earth would never get pollution data.

In this case, researchers may be able to argue that disclosing the information could jeopardise future planned research, for instance by drying up funds from cancer charities. But Graham's tough line with CRU suggests that argument is not guaranteed to succeed.

One reason scientists have such a problem with FOI is that virtually none of them realised that it would apply to them. Certainly, the science community failed to consider the consequences or lobby for the drafting of laws that might make sense for them. Only now is the Royal Society trying to catch up by forming a working group to discuss openness in science.

It is also true that there is little consistency among scientists about what the rules on data sharing and confidentiality should be. Some peer-reviewed journals have tough rules requiring access to that data underpinning research papers, but others do not, including some academic institutions. But there is a growing move to more openness that should surely be welcomed. Cameron Neylon, a biophysicist at the Rutherford Appleton Laboratory in Oxfordshire, writing in *New Scientist* in September, said the aim should be for 'anyone, anywhere to contribute to science'. You can hear the shudders in the labs across the land. But to those who fear an avalanche of ill-informed nonsense arising from data sharing, he said: 'If you care about the place of science in society or are worried about the quality of information on the web, then openness offers massive potential to engage people more deeply, educate them about how science works and increase the store of quality information on the web.'

In the months after climategate there was much discussion in the science community about the need for greater openness. But outside those in the open access movement, it has faltered. The message in the labs is that the inquiries into the affair absolved the scientists of any wrongdoing.

Climate change campaigner, Parliament Square, London, May Day 2010
Credit: Jenny Matthews/Panos

That is not quite true. The inquiries decided, rightly, that there was no grand conspiracy, although they felt they were not in a position to judge the finer points about the conduct of the science. The main enquiry, under Sir Muir Russell, seemed particularly confused about FOI. It noted damagingly that CRU had shown a 'consistent pattern of failing to display the proper degree of openness'. But on the detail it showed a sometimes breathtaking lack of attention. It concluded that 'there was no attempt to delete information with respect to an [FOI] request already made', when the emails published online revealed quite clearly that one round-robin requesting the deletion of an email correspondence was sent two days after an FOI request for precisely that information.

Much of science has 'closed ranks' behind the idea that those demanding access to their data are troublemakers. Nobel laureate and Royal Society president Sir Paul Nurse says 'some researchers … are getting lots of requests for, among other things, all drafts of scientific papers prior to their publication in journals, with annotations, explaining why changes were made between successive versions. If it is true, it will consume a huge amount of time. And it's intimidating.' Maybe, but the current law allows vexatious requests to be rejected. So that is a straw man.

In any event, the whole point of research is that it should be open to maximum scrutiny. And the scientific priesthood can no longer claim that scrutiny should only be among their specialist fellows.

And there is sometimes a fine line between the crackpot and the sublime. Earth science guru Jim Lovelock – a doyen for many modern climate researchers – left institutional academia in frustration at his ideas being ostracised. The *Independent* began its report of the 2011 winner of the Nobel prize for chemistry, Daniel Shechtman, thus: 'An Israeli scientist who was once asked to resign his research post because his discovery of a new class of solid material was too unbelievable has won this year's Nobel Prize in Chemistry – for that same discovery.'

The charge of sloppiness in the way science often portrays its findings to the wider public is also a warning against allowing too much self-policing. In June, the Intergovernmental Panel on Climate Change issued what it said was a summary of the findings of a detailed study of renewable energy. It headlined the claim that 77 per cent of the world's energy needs could be met from green power by 2050. In fact, the '77 per cent' finding was the most optimistic of hundreds of academic studies reviewed in the report itself. Moreover, that particular study was conducted by one of the report's own lead authors, who was also a Greenpeace campaigner. Curious. But most damagingly of all, this highly relevant information only emerged a month after the press release and subsequent media coverage, when IPCC got round to publishing the report itself. This was shameful spin.

The fuss over climategate showed that the world is increasingly unwilling to accept the message that 'we are scientists; trust us'. Other people want to join the scientific conversation. Good scientists, interested in finding truth, should want to encourage them, not put up the shutters. The wider world instinctively knows to distrust those in all walks of life who reject openness. As McIntyre put it recently, 'probably no single issue damages the reputation of the climate science community more than the refusal to show the data that supports their work'. There should, for the good of science as well as public discourse, be a presumption in favour of open access.

McIntyre, meanwhile, is still hunting. He believes CRU researchers using tree rings to unpick temperatures in past eras may have been cherry-picking their Siberian logs to help sustain the argument that recent decades are warmer than anything in the past 2,000 years. He cannot be sure, because they are still refusing to hand over their full data sets. CRU's justifications have a familiar ring. Disclosure could do 'financial harm' to the university by reducing its 'ability to attract research funding'. Really?

If McIntyre eventually gets the data, could it undermine the case that man is warming the world? Certainly not; that is independent of past natural variability. Could it change our ideas about past natural climate change? Conceivably, yes. Is it a scandal that McIntyre cannot get to see the data to review CRU's work and do his own science? I believe it is. ❒

©Fred Pearce
40(4): 113/119
DOI: 10.1177/0306422011428392
www.indexoncensorship.org

Fred Pearce is author of *The Climate Files: The Battle for the Truth about Global Warming* (Guardian Books)

SHOOTING THE MESSENGER

Michael Halpern has concerns that freedom of information requests are open to abuse

Climate scientists report harassment that ranges from the mild to the truly frightening. Radio talk-show hosts in the US subject them to ridicule. Members of Congress looking to score political points hold show trials disguised as hearings and use their platform to cast doubt on scientists' research. Angry partisans send threatening emails and leave vitriolic voicemail messages. One scientist even answered his doorbell to find a dead rat outside the door.

But despite this intense public scrutiny, most scientists had always assumed that their personal conversations and correspondence were sacrosanct. In the privacy of their labs, they felt free to come up with new theories, many of which wouldn't pan out, but a few of which would advance human understanding of the world around us. They felt free to openly challenge their colleagues' ideas to help refine them. They felt free to use scientific terminology with each other without fear that it would be misinterpreted in public at a later date. In short, they felt confident that they had the right to pursue science in a free and unfettered way.

Scientists are not as sure of this right today. As critics of their research try multiple methods to access their correspondence, scientists must rethink what they put in writing, and their institutions must devise ways to protect their ability to have frank discussions with each other. At stake is the ability of researchers to take the risks necessary for scientific progress.

In the US, the climate scientist Michael Mann, whose email correspondence with the University of East Anglia was hacked into two years ago, is still facing serial requests for his data and correspondence. Mann's scientific data and methods have long been publicly available on his personal website. Multiple lines of subsequent research have also confirmed Mann's findings. But that has not stopped those who disagree with the science from going after him in other ways.

On 23 April 2010, Attorney General Ken Cuccinelli, the lead attorney for the Commonwealth of Virginia, served the University of Virginia with a civil investigative demand – in essence a subpoena – for all documents in the university's possession produced by Mann when he was a professor there between 1999 and 2005. The subpoena sought not only data and research methods (which were already publicly available) but also all emails and even handwritten notes in the university's possession.

Together with the American Association of University Professors (AAUP), the Union of Concerned Scientists (UCS) organised a letter signed by more than 800 Virginia scientists and academics urging the university to resist Cuccinelli's demands. Even climate sceptics such as Thomas Fuller objected to the investigation. He wrote an open letter to Cuccinelli:

> No matter what has prompted your investigation, there is no doubt that it will be interpreted as a witch hunt. If you are in fact investigating a credentialed scientist for results that do not suit your political opinion, that interpretation is correct. Unless you can reveal to the public prima facie evidence that shows cause for this investigation, I beg you to reconsider. There are ample avenues of professional and academic recourse for people like me who think he has done something wrong. But being wrong is not a crime, and intimidating scientists not a path that this country, including I presume Virginians, should ever pursue. You may consult with colleagues in Salem to determine how long it takes to live this type of thing down.

The university, which initially seemed poised to comply with the subpoena, did an about face and took the attorney general to court. UCS joined three other organisations in an amicus brief supporting its move, and in August 2010, a circuit court judge sided with the university, telling the attorney general that he was welcome to submit subpoenas, but for them to be enforced he had to demonstrate reason to believe that fraud may have been committed.

The attorney general has continued to beat the deadest of dead horses, submitting similar subpoenas to the university and appealing the judge's decision to the Virginia Supreme Court. Thus far, the cost of the investigation to the university has run into hundreds of thousands of dollars. The court is expected to consider the case in winter 2011; updates will be posted at www.ucsusa.org/cuccinelli.

Next on the scene was the American Tradition Institute (ATI), which seems to want to make it a tradition to attack scientists through open records laws. One of the group's lead spokespeople is Chris Horner, who wrote a book in 2008 called *Red Hot Lies: How Global Warming Alarmists Use Threats, Fraud, and Deception to Keep You Misinformed.*

In January 2011, ATI submitted a request under the Virginia Freedom of Information Act (FOIA) seeking the same broad range of records as the attorney general's subpoena: emails, handwritten notes and any other communication associated with Mann's tenure at the university. ATI was informed that it would be charged $8,500 for the request due to the labour involved in compliance; no payment was submitted. At first glance, it seemed to be a publicity stunt.

In April, along with a dozen other organisations, UCS wrote a letter to the university's president urging the university to '[balance] the interests in public disclosure against the public interest in academic freedom' when complying with the FOIA request. Seven days later, the university pledged to use 'all available exemptions' in its response.

Then the university changed course, entering into a court agreement that seemed counter to the spirit of its pledge. The court agreement gave ATI the right to review all documents – both those that will be eventually released and those that will be withheld – in court under a gag order. In other words, ATI would get to see every single document it requested, even if the material is exempt from ATI's FOIA request.

Now if I were to submit a FOIA request for, say, all of Attorney General Cuccinelli's emails, most or all of my request would likely be denied. I wouldn't expect to be able to go into a judge's chambers and review every email the attorney general had sent. So why would ATI get special treatment?

On 10 August, UCS and other organisations wrote again to the university president to urge it to alter the agreement. After a spate of press-highlighted problems with the agreement, a group of climate scientists started a legal defence fund on behalf of Mann. And a couple of weeks before the university was scheduled to hand over the additional documents, Mann's attorney filed a motion to intervene in the agreement between the university and ATI. The university again changed course and asked a judge to alter the agreement. On 1 November, the judge granted Mann standing in the case and voided the ATI/UVA agreement, instructing them to agree on a neutral third party who will determine what should be disclosed and what shall be considered exempt. The decision keeps thousands of pieces of exempt personal correspondence out of ATI's hands.

There are, of course, advantages to the harassers in pursuing these sorts of FOIA requests. Those who deny the scientific consensus on climate change continue to have a platform to cast doubt on the robustness of the science. When universities resist releasing all of a researcher's private correspondence, it can be alleged that the university must be hiding something scandalous. Meanwhile, legal costs for both the university and the scientists mount.

Open records laws are essential to a functioning democracy. People must be able to have access to information that allows them to keep their government accountable and honest. At the same time, these laws should not be used to chill speech. A well-designed law will create the space for scientists to have frank, private conversations while maintaining the right of the people to understand how their tax dollars are spent.

There are several steps that can be taken to strike this balance. First, academics should be more thoughtful about how their communications can be misrepresented. When academics started using email in the 90s, there was an assumption that sending an email to a colleague was like sending them a letter. Nobody expected the government to go snooping in his or her mailbox. As a result, many scientists expressed frustration with their adversaries that were never intended for public consumption.

Second, open records laws should be scrutinised. In the United States, these laws were first created in the 60s and have been periodically updated. In the wake of the attacks on academic speech, state legislators and FOIA advisory committees should examine whether laws are adequately protective of academics' free speech rights and update them as needed. Third, all universities should be better prepared to respond to subpoenas and FOIA requests.

With safeguards in place, scientists will feel safe asking tough questions of their peers, especially when their research touches upon contentious issues. Those who have the courage to present ideas that challenge the status quo will be supported. And those who feel threatened by scientific progress will not be able to use these tools to slow it down. ❐

©Michael Halpern
40(4): 120/123
DOI: 10.1177/0306422011428393
www.indexoncensorship.org

Michael Halpern is Program Manager of the Scientific Integrity Program at the Union of Concerned Scientists

SMOG RULES

Is President Obama putting corporate interests ahead of those of the planet? **Rick Piltz** reports on a retreat from good intentions

Very early in his presidency, in March 2009, President Obama made a strong statement to the federal agencies about the need to protect scientific integrity in government. This was in welcome contrast with, and surely in part a response to, the political interference that federal scientists and science communication suffered under the previous administration. But has Obama made good on his commitment?

In the arena of climate science and policy, the government of George W Bush engaged in avoidance, misrepresentation and censorship of communication about global warming, its causes and implications – well documented in investigations by the House Committee on Oversight and Government Reform, the Union of Concerned Scientists and the Government Accountability Project. While no comparably intensive investigations have been carried out during the past three years, the widespread chilling effect on federal climate science communication does not appear to have continued under Obama.

In contrast with the situation under Bush, the Obama administration's position on climate change is not in conflict with the overall message of

BP Deepwater Horizon oil spill, Gulf of Mexico, Louisiana, USA, 20 June 2010
Credit: Jim McKinley/Alamy

March against mountaintop removal coal mining, West Virginia, USA, 10 June 2011
Credit: Jim West/Alamy

climate science, as articulated in the conclusions of the scientific assessments by the Intergovernmental Panel on Climate Change (IPCC) and reports by the National Academy of Sciences. Leading administration officials, including science adviser John Holdren, Energy Secretary Steven Chu and Jane Lubchenco, head of the National Oceanic and Atmospheric Administration, scientists all, have spoken about climate change and the need for a strong climate policy.

At the same time, we have seen much of the Republican Party in denial about the reality, or at least the seriousness, of human-caused global warming and of the importance of taking action to mitigate or adapt to climate change. The campaign of climate change disinformation, developed during the past two decades by anti-regulatory corporate interests and 'free market' policy groups, has been embraced by the party's right-wing base and has become something of a litmus test for support for Republican congressional candidates, and now for those jostling for the party's presidential nomination in 2012.

During 2011, the Republicans in the House of Representatives held a series of hearings and staged a series of votes that amounted to a kind of declaration of war on the climate science community. They approved legislation, thus far blocked in the Senate, seeking to prohibit the Environmental Protection Agency from promulgating science-based regulation of greenhouse gases as a threat to public health and welfare. One vote explicitly rejected language that would have acknowledged the scientific conclusion that human activity is changing the global climate. Another vote would have eliminated US funding for the IPCC assessments. The science journal *Nature* editorialised on 16 March: 'It is hard to escape the conclusion that the US Congress has entered the intellectual wilderness, a sad state of affairs in a country that has led the world in many scientific arenas for so long.'

So the Obama administration has managed to look rather good in comparison, simply by not joining in the rejection of climate science and attacks on the integrity of leading climate scientists. But the measure of the administration's performance should involve more than whether it has cleared this very low bar. Obama created high expectations, and the public interest calls for them to be met. In these terms, there remain significant unanswered questions about the strength and limits of federal scientific integrity policy, especially in cases when the science might be inconvenient for policymaking and political messaging.

In his March 2009 memorandum on scientific integrity, Obama directed his White House science adviser, John Holdren, to consult with the heads of executive departments and agencies and gave him four months, to July, to make recommendations for presidential action to guarantee scientific integrity and the integrity of the relationship between science and policymaking throughout the federal government. However, the July deadline passed, and a process internal to the administration continued for another 17 months. Holdren, a Harvard University professor and now director of the White House Office of Science and Technology Policy (OSTP), finally issued another statement to the agencies in December 2010. Just four pages long, it recommended a general framework for the development of scientific integrity policies on an agency-by-agency basis. It contained no recommendations for presidential action and put forward no deadlines. By August 2011, of 19 relevant agencies, only five had submitted completed policy statements, and another 14 had submitted drafts that were in various stages. Most of the draft policies were not made available for public review and comment. Thus the process dragged on.

In the handful of cases in which the agencies' scientific integrity policies were available for review, there tended to be all-too-evident shortcomings in some key areas. Typically, they did not really ensure that federal scientists would be protected from interference by political appointees and supervisors. Media policies did not fully remove political barriers, actual and perceived, to freedom of communication between scientists and journalists and the dissemination of scientific information to the public. Policies lacked explicit whistleblower protections and failed to specify procedural safeguards to protect agency scientists and other employees who report scientific misconduct or political interference with research. The process of developing and implementing the policies lacked transparency and accountability.

A survey of journalists reported in the September/October 2011 issue of the *Columbia Journalism Review*, and a subsequent discussion by a cross-section of science journalists held at the National Press Club in Washington, DC, revealed that reporters still face unresponsive agency public information offices, intrusive monitoring of interviews with government scientists and long delays in the processing of requests under the Freedom of Information Act (FOIA).

Why do these problems persist, and why has it taken years for the federal agencies to adopt scientific integrity policies? Granted, the agencies faced the challenge of developing new policy to specify the terms of 'scientific integrity' within the complex federal arena. But it appeared that political factors came into play to delay and weaken the effort. Where was the obstruction located? The most likely explanation lay not in the OSTP but in a combination of bureaucratic foot-dragging by agency officials reluctant to commit to greater openness and transparency and the controlling hand of the powerful White House Office of Management and Budget (OMB).

A very limited set of documents released in response to a FOIA lawsuit filed by the advocacy group Public Employees for Environmental Responsibility, seeking to shed light on the reasons for the delay, suggested that OMB had approval authority over the guidelines and was using it to delay and constrain the process. OMB not only controls agency budgets, it also exercises authority given to it by successive presidents to approve, disapprove and shape proposed new federal regulations, including science-based regulations, and has extensive authority over federal collection and dissemination of information. OMB, while not having appreciable in-house scientific expertise, in effect exercises considerable authority over the use of science in policy-making. As environmental journalist Joseph A Davis has noted: 'For decades, under both Democratic and Republican

STOP THE PIPELINE

President of Friends of the Earth, right, speaks in front of federal court with Noah Greenwood from the Center for Biological Diversity, 5 October 2011, Omaha, Nebraska. Conservation groups are filing a lawsuit against TransCanada's Keystone XL pipeline. Credit: Nati Harnik/AP Photo

administrations, OMB has held and used the authority to overrule scientific findings and set agency regulations from the White House, based on secret meetings with industry groups that contribute major money to presidential campaigns.' If an administration finds science to be a potential impediment to a politically preferred course of action, there are ways to get around it.

On 18 July 2011, the Department of the Interior suspended federal wildlife biologist Charles Monnett, whose 2006 report on sightings of drowned polar bears in Arctic waters, published in the journal *Polar Biology*, had been given prominent attention, including in Al Gore's film *An Inconvenient Truth*. Dr Monnett, a career scientist in the department's Bureau of Ocean Energy Management, Regulation and Enforcement, was informed that he was under investigation for 'integrity issues'. Investigators seized his computer hard drive and notebooks and he was grilled at length on his 2006 report by his department's inspector general.

Monnett's report was the first time scientists had suggested a connection between the melting of sea ice and an increased risk of polar bear mortality. Polar bears depend on sea ice for their survival, and receding ice requires adult bears and cubs to swim greater distances. After a thorough scientific review of many studies, in 2008 the polar bear was formally listed by the Interior Department as 'threatened' under the terms of the Endangered Species Act, based on the projected disappearance of its sea-ice habitat during the next few decades under conditions of global warming.

Monnett co-ordinated a $50m portfolio of research supported by his agency on Arctic wildlife and ecology. His investigators raised questions about alleged irregularities in connection with the funding of a joint US-Canadian study of polar bear population movements in response to changing ice conditions. Inexplicably, the researchers in that study were hit with a temporary stop-work order on 13 July 2011, a few days before Monnett was suspended.

Public Employees for Environmental Responsibility (Peer) represented and vigorously defended Monnett against what it referred to as harassment based on 'a mixture of false assumptions, misinformation and some just plain nutty notions'. Peer's executive director questioned Monnett being 'suspended just now as an arm of the Interior Department is getting ready to make its decision on offshore drilling in the Arctic seas'. Peer filed a formal scientific misconduct complaint against Interior Department officials. Greenpeace and the Center for Biological Diversity also raised with the White House and the Interior Department the issue of whether the Monnett case violated the terms of his department's new scientific integrity policy to protect scientists from political interference. Monnett was reported as saying in an interview transcript that his superiors 'don't want any impediment to, you know, what they view as their mission, which is to, you know, drill wells up there' and 'put areas into production'.

The Monnett case appeared to collapse and he returned to work on 26 August, after six weeks on leave. His bureau was informed that its top officials, including the director, an Obama appointee, were themselves being investigated by Interior's Scientific Integrity Officer, following Peer's scientific misconduct complaint. This suggests that formal scientific integrity policy, at least when combined with public interest pressure and bad publicity, can be used to push back on political interference with research.

On the other hand, while Monnett was under suspension, the Interior Department conditionally approved Royal Dutch Shell's application to begin exploring for oil in the Arctic Ocean in the summer of 2012. This signalled that the administration had decided to resume support for offshore drilling under potentially very hazardous conditions, which had been put on hold following the disastrous BP Deepwater Horizon oil blowout in the Gulf of Mexico in 2010. In what has been termed an 'approve-then-verify' approach to exploration plans, the government appeared to accept Shell's claim that it could recover 90 per cent of any oil in freezing Arctic waters after a blowout, which could potentially continue uncontrolled for many months.

Is drilling for oil in the Arctic Ocean another disaster waiting to happen? Does the decision to begin permitting offshore drilling in the Arctic simply establish a fait accompli vis-à-vis unresolved scientific concerns about environmental impacts – ie science not censored but rather set aside, in order to expedite production and fend off industry complaints about environmental reviews?

Blocking the smog rule may set a dangerous precedent

On 2 September 2011, Obama rejected a proposed Environmental Protection Agency (EPA) regulation under the Clean Air Act that would have set a scientifically-based health standard requiring substantial reductions in emissions of smog-causing pollutants. The new rule, following the recommendations of EPA science advisers, would have strengthened a weaker standard set at the end of the Bush administration. Ground-level ozone pollution, or smog, can cause lung damage, breathing difficulties and heart problems. The EPA's own analysis had found that the health benefits of the proposed new standard would outweigh industry's regulatory compliance costs. EPA administrator Lisa Jackson had made pushing through a tough new clean air standard for ozone one of the key initiatives of her tenure. That initiative is now on hold until after the 2012 presidential election.

Notwithstanding the Clean Air Act requirement that the EPA set a health and science-based standard, with economic costs to be considered only at the stage of state-level implementation plans, the White House decision to direct the EPA to pull down its smog rule did not pretend to be based on science. In fact, it flew in the face of the scientific evidence on the health effects of ozone pollution. Rather, Obama sided with Republican and industry complaints that the smog rule would impose a costly regulatory burden and hinder job creation under conditions of high unemployment and a shaky economic recovery. Thus, he capitulated to the 'environment versus jobs' framing, lending legitimacy to the view that pits the economy against public health and environmental protection. The president of the American Petroleum Institute, the chief lobbying arm of the US oil industry, praised the decision.

The *Wall Street Journal* reported that the Office of Management and Budget regulatory czar Cass Sunstein and White House Chief of Staff William Daley had teamed up to kill the smog rule. A record of meetings on the OMB website reveals that, on 16 August 2011, Sunstein, Daley and other White House officials met with representatives of the US Chamber of Commerce, the American Chemistry Council, the National Petrochemical and Refiners Association, the American Petroleum Institute, the National Association of Manufacturers, the American Forest and Paper Association and the Business Roundtable to discuss reconsideration of the ozone air quality standard – just 17 days before Obama rejected the new rule. While the Clean Air Act assigns statutory authority to promulgate air quality standards to the EPA – not to the OMB or White House political staff – the EPA was clearly outgunned in this company. While EPA administrator Jackson would be considered a hero by many environmentalists if she were to defy the White House, or resign in protest, US politics has no real tradition of principled and outspoken resignations by cabinet officials.

An anti-regulatory agenda that is always present is being pushed in effect to take advantage of a president who has been all-too-willing to accommodate corporate pressure. The smog rule is one of several new regulations pulled back by the administration after corporate interests complained they would hinder job creation. Congressional Republicans have been emboldened to make a radical demand for a moratorium on all federal regulations.

The decision to block the smog rule may set a dangerous precedent for other environmental policy decisions with a significant scientific component, including decisions relevant to climate change and energy development. For example, what will happen to the EPA's forthcoming rulemaking on reducing carbon-dioxide emissions from power plants – scheduled to be made final in 2012 – in the heat of the election campaign? The EPA announced in

September that it would not meet a 30 September deadline for submitting the proposed power plant rule, currently under development, for consideration by OMB – where it could be weakened and further delayed, perhaps until after the next election.

Meanwhile, the administration moves ahead with a likely presidential decision to approve construction of the proposed 1700-mile Keystone XL pipeline, designed to carry Canadian tar sands oil from Alberta to refineries on the Texas Gulf Coast. Will Obama heed the letter sent to him by James Hansen and other leading climate scientists, which said: 'Adding [the tar sands] on top of conventional fossil fuels will leave our children and grand-children a climate system with consequences that are out of their control. . . . [W]e can say categorically that [the pipeline is] not only not in the national interest, it's also not in the planet's best interest.'

Climate scientists continue to publish their research and communicate their findings, though they now face the prospect of substantial cuts to funding of research and observing systems in coming years under the demand for federal fiscal austerity. But in the collision between climate science and the realities of Washington politics, science gets muscled aside by the relentless pressure to expedite further development of fossil fuel resources regardless of environmental and scientific concerns – deepwater drilling for oil in the Gulf of Mexico, offshore drilling in the Arctic Ocean, exploitation of the Canadian tar sands, mountaintop removal coal mining that has laid waste to large areas of Appalachia and hydraulic fracturing to develop natural gas from shale rock formations.

'The lamentable truth,' said *Nature* in a 15 September editorial on how science and the environment appear to be taking a back seat in Obama's campaign for re-election, 'is that in the world of US politics, environmental protection is still debated as if it were an optional and expensive accessory to modern living. In the process, science is set aside.' ❐

©Rick Piltz
40(4): 124/133
DOI: 10.1177/0306422011428247
www.indexoncensorship.org

Rick Piltz is the director of Climate Science Watch, a public interest watchdog project in Washington, DC, sponsored by the Government Accountability Project

ARTICLES OF FAITH

Medical journals are no longer fit for purpose and bestow credibility on research that often does not deserve it, argues **Richard Smith**

Medical journals, the main way in which medical research reaches both doctors and the public, are a corrupted form of communication. That's the melancholic conclusion I reached after 25 years as an editor on the *BMJ* (formerly the *British Medical Journal*) and two months in a 15th-century palazzo in Venice in 2003 writing a book. *The Trouble with Medical Journals* was published in 2006. So, five years later, are things better or worse?

The premise for my book was that medical journals were over-influenced by the pharmaceutical industry, too fond of the mass media, and yet neglectful of patients. The research they contained was hard to interpret and prone to bias, while peer review, the process at the heart of journals and all of science, was deeply flawed. Many of the studies journals contained were fraudulent, and yet the scientific community had not responded adequately to the problem of fraud. Editors themselves also misbehaved. The authors of the studies in journals often had little to do with the work they were reporting and many had conflicts of interest that were not declared. And the whole business of medical journals was corrupt because owners were making money from restricting access to important research, most of it funded by

public money. All this matters to everybody because medical journals have a strong influence on their healthcare and lives.

For 13 of my years at the *BMJ* I was both its editor and chief executive of the BMJ Publishing Group, which publishes a stable of journals and does much else. Since I left, in 2004, I have continued to write for journals, blog weekly for the *BMJ*, and serve on the board of the Public Library of Science (PLoS), a not-for-profit organisation that aims to make all scientific research 'open access', meaning both that it can be accessed by anybody for free and reused without having to ask permission. In the longer term, PloS wants to reinvent the publishing of science, believing that discoveries should be disseminated more quickly and effectively. It already publishes several journals, including *PloS Medicine*, which began in 2004, and the revolutionary *PloS One*, which began in 2006, of which more later. So, despite my disillusionment with medical journals I continue to be heavily involved with them. This is not entirely hypocritical because they are, for now, the best place for doctors, scientists and others to debate medicine and science.

Yet it is common for articles in journals to be scientifically poor, while some have been profoundly flawed and caused great harm. By far and away the best example of this is the notorious article by Andrew Wakefield and others published in the *Lancet* in 1998 that linked the MMR (measles, mumps, rubella) vaccine to autism. The idea took hold, and many parents decided not to have their children vaccinated, leading to outbreaks of measles.

The original *Lancet* paper described a series of 12 cases where there seemed to be a link between children developing a bowel disorder and autism and having been given the MMR vaccine. The study was scientifically very weak and was strongly criticised. A series of subsequent papers by other scientists did not find any link. In 2004, following an investigation by the journalist Brian Deer, it emerged that Wakefield had been paid by lawyers to establish whether there was a link between the vaccine and autism. He had not declared this conflict of interest and Richard Horton, the editor of the *Lancet*, said that he would not have published the study if he had known about it. Subsequently, ten of the 13 authors of the study retracted its interpretation that there was any link between the vaccine and autism. Wakefield has denied any wrongdoing.

The story may well have further to go. After Deer's investigation, Wakefield and a colleague appeared before the General Medical Council (GMC), which regulates British doctors, in one of its longest-running cases. In 2010, both doctors were found guilty of serious professional misconduct and struck off the medical register. Wakefield was found guilty of dishonesty

and causing children to be subjected to invasive procedures that were clinically unjustified. Both doctors have appealed the judgment to the High Court.

Deer continued his investigations, and this year published three important articles in the *BMJ*. The first argues that the original study was not
simply unethical, the main finding of the GMC, but fraudulent, with many
dishonest claims being made about the cases. The second article reveals
Wakefield's plans for a potentially lucrative commercial deal for his research,
and the third article, in many ways the most troubling, argues that the *Lancet*
conducted a rapid and inadequate investigation when serious accusations
about the original paper were brought to it by Deer in 2004. Fiona Godlee,
the editor of the *BMJ*, wrote about Deer's allegation: 'It is hard to escape
the conclusion that this represents institutional and editorial misconduct.'

The world of full-time medical editors is small, and Godlee and Horton
have known each other for years. Godlee thought long and hard before
publishing the article about the *Lancet* and concluded that a journal ought
to be willing to criticise anybody, including its friends, when necessary.
Interestingly, the *Lancet* has never responded publicly to the *BMJ* article
and, as far as I know, the *Lancet*'s owners are not conducting an inquiry. Is
this an example of editorial misconduct?

Some of the best researchers may have misbehaved

What this sorry episode illustrates is that you cannot automatically trust
the material that appears in medical journals – it may be scientifically weak
or even fraudulent. Since my book was published there have been many
examples of fraud. Indeed, in September, the *Economist* told the story of
a group from Duke University in North Carolina who published a study in
the *New England Journal of Medicine*, the world's leading medical journal,
describing how they could predict the course of a patient's lung cancer
using genetic techniques. Soon after they published another study, in *Nature
Medicine*, of using genetic techniques to predict which cancers in individuals would respond to chemotherapy. These were important developments,
and other groups tried to replicate the work. They couldn't and discovered

many errors in the original studies. Duke University was asked to investigate but found no problems. Then it emerged that one of the Duke researchers had lied about his qualifications, including that he had been a Rhodes scholar in Australia. (It was odd that nobody picked up on this earlier as Rhodes scholars all go to Oxford.) At this point everything unravelled, and the studies have since been retracted – meaning that they should be ignored.

Unfortunately this sort of story is very familiar. Universities naturally find it very uncomfortable to think that some of their best researchers may have misbehaved and tend to be slow to investigate and too quick to find 'no problem'. That inevitable conflict of interest was compounded in this case by the university having ties with companies that the researchers were involved with. The journals were also reluctant to publish criticisms of the studies, and those who did criticise the work had to publish their findings in less high-profile journals.

The *Economist* concludes its piece with the observation that 'the episode does serve as a timely reminder of one thing that is sometimes forgotten. Scientists are human, too'. I've long argued that we may have such difficulty managing misconduct in science because we cling to the idea that science is an objective activity and somehow not prey to the human failings that are seen in every other walk of life. It is, of course, a human activity carried out by human beings, and so there will be misconduct. Indeed, because the stakes can be so high and the controls so poor there may be more misconduct in science than in many other spheres.

Daniele Fanelli, from Edinburgh University, systematically reviewed 21 studies that asked scientists about misconduct in 2009 and found that 2 per cent admitted having fabricated, falsified, or modified data at least once and 14 per cent said that they knew of colleagues doing so. These are serious offences. The review also looked at 'questionable research practices' (things such as intentional non-publication of results, biased methodology and misleading reporting) and found that 34 per cent of researchers admitted to these and 72 per cent thought that their colleagues had been guilty of them.

The review did not consider plagiarism and professional misconduct (things such as guest authorship and failing to declare conflicts of interest), but the results are staggering, even terrifying. If they are to be believed – and they come, remember, from a systematic review of many studies – then there may be profound corruption of the scientific record. Many have argued that it is the common minor distortions, the 'questionable research practices', that cause more harm than the high-profile cases of fabrication and plagiarism.

5-7 McPHERSO

The response of the scientific community to research misconduct has been weak. Many countries have no system at all for preventing and responding to research misconduct, and the British story is one of procrastination and obfuscation. For a long time scientific leaders in Britain argued that the problem was small (without any evidence at all), little harm was done and science was in any case self-correcting. But at a meeting of leaders in medical research in Edinburgh in 1999 it was agreed that something had to be done. Nothing happened until a few people who were deeply concerned managed to set up the UK Panel for Research Integrity in Health and Biomedical Sciences in 2006, now known as the UK Research Integrity Office (UKRIO).

I am a member of UKRIO and, as our legally qualified chairman told us, we have the legal status of a 'cricket club' – in other words, we are a group of people who have come together concerned about an issue but with no legal powers to investigate or enforce anything. We can advise and support but little more. This has caused many critics to describe UKRIO as 'toothless' and hence ineffective. The organisation has certainly had a shaky history. It began slowly, and last year the UK Research Councils and Universities UK decided that they would no longer support it financially and would eventually – after an interregnum – start their own organisation. UKRIO was not against a new organisation but was highly sceptical that any new body would actually appear. It feared that the image of UK science would be damaged by having taken two decades to set up any kind of body and then disbanding it after a few years. So UKRIO has continued, seeking funding from individual universities.

Although it is 'toothless', it is probably the best kind of institution for Britain at the moment. Universities, where most research is done, are very keen to preserve their independence and resist strongly a body that would have statutory powers to investigate and, if necessary, punish them. They are, however, open to support and advice, and it may be that if most universities do join UKRIO then it will be embarrassing not to belong – and that the power of peer pressure to be serious about research misconduct may be more effective than new laws.

While national scientific authorities have been slow to respond to misconduct, journals have done much better. I was a founder member of the Committee on Publication Ethics (Cope) in 1997, and we began as a small self-help group for editors, helping each other respond to the many ethical problems editors faced once they chose to recognise them. At the *BMJ* we underwent a transformation from thinking that ethical and misconduct issues in papers submitted to the journal but not accepted by us (about 90 per cent of those submitted) were not our problem, to recognising that we had a duty to act. The result was that we went from dealing with one or two cases a year to dealing with perhaps 20.

Cope now has some 7,000 members from across the world, including many non-medical journals. It has full-time staff, a code of conduct and guidelines on ethical issues and holds seminars around the world and funds research. It has dealt with over 400 cases of misconduct and has a database of them all.

There is still, however, a considerable mismatch between the scale of the problem of misconduct, as shown by the systematic review, and the response. We might expect universities to be dealing with dozens of cases, not just a handful, and hundreds of 'retractions' of articles. Retraction of a study means that it can no longer be trusted. Retraction of an article is signalled on databases such as PubMed although, ironically, retracted articles tend to be cited just as often as those that are not retracted, showing how sloppy people are in their 'scholarship'.

Retractions of articles have increased sharply since 1980, but only about 0.02 per cent of articles are retracted – and only a third of those for misconduct. We have to worry that there are many more studies that should be retracted, but retraction is embarrassing for authors, editors, journals, publishers and funders. The temptation to turn a blind eye is huge.

Interestingly, higher profile journals have higher rates of retraction. Why? Nobody knows for sure, but it might well be that those journals have more staff and more resources to work through the complex process of organising a retraction. But it might also be that those journals are attracted to the new, exciting and sexy, the very characteristics that fraudsters are trying to achieve.

Journals may be attracted to the exciting and sexy

One of the biggest insights I have gained into journals since I wrote my book came from a paper published in *PLoS Medicine* that described the 'winner's curse'. This is an economic concept that says that in a bidding process the person who wins may well have overbid, promising too much or offering too low a price. Those who regularly make bids recognise the problem and may reduce the attractiveness of their bid, and those who select bids may ignore the ones that seem most attractive. John Ioannidis, a brilliant researcher who has done more than anybody to identify serious problems with the publishing of science, was one of the authors of the paper, and the implication is that the top journals, which fight hard for the most important papers, may well be filled with papers suffering from the winner's curse. This might explain the higher rate of retraction.

Ioannidis and his colleagues have some evidence to support their hypothesis. A study from the *Journal of the American Medical Association* (*JAMA*) showed that of the 49 most highly cited papers on medical interventions published in high-profile journals between 1990 and 2004, a quarter of the randomised trials and five of six non-randomised studies had been contradicted or found to be exaggerated by 2005. A second study looked at original studies of biomarkers with 400 citations or more from 24 highly cited journals. These studies were compared with subsequent meta-analyses that evaluated the same biomarkers, and of the 35 highly cited original studies, 29 showed an effect size larger than that in the meta-analyses. What this means is that if people are reading only top journals – *Nature*, *Science*, *Cell*, *New England Journal of Medicine*, *Lancet*, *JAMA*, *BMJ* – they are getting a distorted view of science. Treatments will seem more effective and diagnostic tests more accurate than they actually are.

This is a profound observation because it undermines the main reason that scientific journals exist. Every year hundreds of thousands of scientific studies are published. These could all be simply put on databases (as is starting to happen), but instead there is an elaborate, expensive and time-consuming process for sorting these papers with the idea that the most important appear in the high-profile journals. In other words, the main value of journals is that they sort the hundreds of thousands of studies – they are, in effect, a device for coping with 'information overload'. The work of Ioannidis and others suggests that far from sorting the information, they are introducing a bias into the system.

The other main function of scientific journals is quality assurance. They do this through peer review, and the implicit promise is that what appears in journals is scientifically sound and can be trusted. In my book, I described the substantial evidence that much of what appears in journals is scientifically weak and expressed my scepticism about peer review. Since then I have reached the conclusion that little would be lost and much gained if we were to abandon what is now called 'pre-publication peer review'.

In the 80s, people began to study peer review and reveal how those studies have failed to show any benefit but have revealed many problems: peer

The heyday of scientific research in the 17th century when peer review took place through open debate
Credit: Science Photo Library

review is slow, expensive ($1.7bn a year), inefficient, wasteful of academic time, largely a lottery, ineffective at spotting error, anti-innovatory and unable to detect fraud. A recent example I have encountered of this concerns an innovatory study that was reviewed by 24 people on behalf of four journals over two years and was eventually published without any important changes.

Distressingly, few scientists and editors are aware of the evidence on peer review, yet many continue to believe in it passionately. Ironically, pre-publication peer review is a faith-based rather than an evidence-based process. What I and others who are sceptical of pre-publication peer review argue is that post-publication peer review has always been the real peer review, in that it decides, ultimately, the importance of a study. By post-publication peer review I don't mean the comments attached to published papers, which are exceedingly sparse, but rather the market of ideas, whereby readers, commentators, journal clubs, systematic reviewers and others digest a study. I fear that the main reason that people stick so enthusiastically to pre-publication peer review is summed up by Upton Sinclair's observation: 'It is difficult to get a man to understand something, when his salary depends upon his not understanding it.'

Were people to accept that pre-publication peer review is worthless and that the sorting of studies by publishing the most important ones in the top journals is actually introducing bias, then the two main pillars of scientific journals collapse. Huge vested interests are opposed to these ideas because journal publishing is a business generating billions of dollars and employing tens of thousands of people.

The newspaper business generates even more income (although perhaps lower profits) and provides more jobs, but it is dying. The *Economist* recently argued that newspapers may prove to be an 'historical aberration' and that news will return to its roots of being spread by word of mouth in markets and taverns – only now it will be spread through the internet. I believe that scientific journals may also prove to be an historical aberration and that the dissemination of science could return to the 17th century when scientists went to meetings and presented their studies. The assembled scientists would then discuss and critique the studies. We can imagine the intensity, energy, and passion of those meetings. This was the original peer review: immediate and open. The same could happen now on a global scale, again through the internet.

One development since I published my book may prove to be a game-changer – that is, the publication of thousands of articles on open access databases after peer review that doesn't ask whether a study is 'important and original' but simply whether the conclusions are supported by the methods and data. *PLoS One* was the first of these, but it has spawned almost a dozen imitators. *PLoS One* has grown dramatically and is now publishing almost a thousand papers a month, making it by far the largest scientific journal in the world (if it can be called a journal).

Scientific journals may prove to be an historical aberration

The reason that so many publishers have copied the idea is not, I fear, because they see it as important for science, but rather that it can be highly profitable. If their journals attract as many papers as *PLoS One* and if the scheme continues to grow at the same rate then it might be that traditional journals begin to disappear. So far this hasn't happened, and some of them continue to be extremely profitable. The profit margins of scientific publishers such as Elsevier and Springer still run at above 30 per cent. The basis of their success is that their most valuable asset – the science – comes for free. Others have paid for it, usually with public money. Interestingly, both the *Guardian* and the *New York Times* have recently run articles critical of the high prices and profits of scientific publishers.

Pressure for open access to research is steadily mounting from funders and universities. Many universities have created open access repositories for studies from their staff (known as 'green open access' in contrast to 'gold open access', which means published in journals), and some traditional journals will allow authors to place their articles in the repositories, which could become alternatives to journals.

There are now nearly 5,000 open access journals and 200,000 open access articles, but in 2009 only 7.7 per cent of articles were gold open access. So 90 per cent of research articles are still locked away behind access controls with the fee for access to a single article usually around $30. I was recently looking for the first piece I ever published in a medical journal – a short letter in the *Lancet* in 1974. It would have cost me $31.50 to access the letter, something like 25 cents for every word.

I have been arguing since the mid-90s that eventually all studies would be open access because the drivers, particularly the financial drivers, are so strong. There are arguments over the economics, but it seems almost certain that all research could be open access through an author-pays (or more correctly institution-pays) model for less than is currently spent on journals. The age of austerity leads to increasing pressure for reform, but so does the drive for economic growth, because the more people who have access to the research the more likely that new products, services and businesses can develop.

The main factor that holds back universal open access is academic credit, which is tied to where people publish. In order to flourish as a scientist you must appear in prestigious journals such as *Nature*, *Science*, *Cell*, *New England Journal of Medicine* and the *Lancet*, none of which are open access journals. Most of the 'second division' of journals are also closed access. PloS tried to end this stranglehold by creating prestigious open access journals, but it has not yet been able to make the breakthrough.

Now, however, three major research funders, including the Wellcome Trust, are planning to launch an open access journal in 2012 that they hope will change the game. The journal, which will compete head on with *Nature*, *Science* and *Cell*, will be edited by scientists rather than 'failed postdocs', as it disparagingly sees professional editors. Peer review and publication will be rapid, reviewers will be paid and everything will be open access. The funders probably have enough money and clout to succeed.

Ironically, attributing credit to academics based on where they publish is unscientific – because the impact factor of a journal (the number of citations divided by the number of citable articles) is driven by a few articles that are highly cited. There is little correlation between the citations of articles in a journal and its impact factor.

It makes much more sense to judge an individual article on its own merits rather than use the journal in which it is published as a surrogate measure of quality. This is now possible because PloS has introduced something called article level metrics. If you click on any article published in a PloS journal you can see the number of views and downloads, a graph of views over time (showing whether the paper is still 'alive'), citations in several databases and other measures of impact. These data are almost in real time and they are a much better way to judge the importance of an academic's paper. These metrics are also a potential gamechanger, but most journals still don't have them – even though the software that PloS uses is open source.

In general, I think that most of the problems surrounding medical journals that I first identified in my book persist today. Perhaps if I take another snapshot in five years' time there will be more improvements, or perhaps journals will have begun to disappear, proving after all to have been nothing more than an 'historical aberration'. ❐

©Richard Smith
40(4): 135/147
DOI: 10.1177/0306422011427790
www.indexoncensorship.org

Richard Smith is director of the United Health Chronic Disease Initiative, a programme to counter chronic disease in the developing world. A board member of the Public Library of Science, he was editor of the *BMJ* and chief executive of the BMJ Publishing Group

LSE *space for thought* LITERARY FESTIVAL

Wednesday 29 February – Saturday 3 March 2012

Relating Cultures

A series of events at the London School of Economics and Political Science (LSE), free and open to all, exploring the relationships between the academic cultures of the arts and social sciences, the interaction between global cultures, and the art of communication and language with award-winning authors and academics.

Justin Cartwright

Claire Tomalin

Jonathan Powell

Elif Shafak

Amit Chaudhuri

John Lanchester

Full details online in December 2011
lse.ac.uk/spaceforthought

WHISTLE STOP

If society wants people to speak out on matters of public concern, it needs to be acceptable to blow the whistle, says **Peter Wilmshurst**

When Dr Stephen Bolsin raised concerns with senior managers about the high death rate for children undergoing cardiac surgery in Bristol, most of the other healthcare professionals who knew of the excess mortality rate remained silent and failed to support him. That was not an isolated case. Without the aberrant intervention of a whistleblower, poor practice in institutions and misconduct by individuals are usually concealed. We need to understand why only a minority of people who are aware of matters of serious public concern, such as patient safety in the National Health Service or misconduct, are prepared to be whistleblowers, and the majority of people collude in a cover-up by self-censoring.

Part of the reason is that most people, even whistleblowers, censor the expression of their own views every day. We may think that another person's clothes demonstrate poor dress sense but we make no comment to avoid giving gratuitous offence to the wearer and precipitating confrontation, because the way people dress is relatively unimportant, is not our business and because we lack confidence in our own opinions. This socially acceptable form of self-censorship about minor matters is considered appropriate.

Because of the social mores that people should mind their own business, be cautious when saying things that might cause offence, be certain of their facts before expressing criticisms and give others the benefit of the doubt, there is often reluctance for people to speak out. We teach our children to mind their own business and avoid gratuitous frankness.

As a result of these mores, it can be difficult for people to decide whether an issue is sufficiently serious to speak out. People can generally convince themselves that they should not get involved and that if the matter is serious enough someone else will report it. The knowledge that whistleblowers are treated badly is also a major incentive for self-censorship.

For much of society, a whistleblower is no different from an informer, and no sector in society likes an informer. They are given derogatory names like snitch, sneak and grass. The name Judas has become synonymous with someone who betrays a friend or colleague. Society generally, and some religions specifically, believe that loyalty is a virtue in its own right, even if the underlying cause is dishonourable. As a result, society tends to shun informers or whistleblowers. There is also an element of self-protection, because we might be concerned that a whistleblower will also inform on us. So whistleblowers face penalties from their peers, institutions, the law and society in general, and these are disincentives for reporting concerns.

Many organisations have codes of conduct that require a member to keep silent about misconduct or bad practice by its members. These codes of conduct may be secret or published. It is no surprise that the mafia has a code of *omertá*. It is more surprising that the General Medical Council (GMC), which regulates and licenses doctors to practise in the UK, has a rule that may impede one doctor raising concerns about another (codified in 'Good Medical Practice', its guidance for doctors). I discovered it when I raised concerns about misconduct by a group of doctors and the initial act of the GMC was to investigate me, the complainant, under its rule prohibiting one doctor from disparaging another. Only when I was cleared did the GMC investigate my complaint, determine that my concerns were justified and issue warnings to the doctors about their future conduct. Although the GMC code also encourages its members to take appropriate steps when they believe that a colleague may not be fit to practise, if a doctor risks facing punishment by the GMC for raising concerns about a colleague, most would consider it prudent to remain silent.

The treatment I received contrasts with the way that the GMC dealt with one of its own senior members, who at the time was the chair of the professional conduct committee (the former name of the committee that adjudicates when a doctor is accused of misconduct) and also the medical director of a hospital in which a doctor was found to have embezzled money from the accounts of a medical charity. A severance agreement between the doctor and the hospital management board agreed not to make the scandal public. As a result, the doctor's criminal activity was concealed. The hospital also destroyed the documentation compiled in its investigation. I reported the doctor to the GMC. The professional conduct committee found him guilty and suspended him from the medical register. The start of the hearing was delayed because the chair of the committee, who had chaired a panel investigating the embezzlement at the hospital, had to stand down from the case and a replacement was appointed. The GMC took no action against the chair, despite requests from me and the GMC's own lawyers. He subsequently returned to hearing other cases. From these two cases we might conclude that the GMC believes that if a doctor reports misconduct by another doctor it is a more serious form of unprofessional behaviour than if a senior doctor fails to report wrongdoing to the GMC.

A code of silence also exists in the police. It was demonstrated by the miscarriage of justice that sent an innocent man, Stefan Kiszko, to prison for 16 years for the sexually motivated murder of schoolgirl Lesley Molseed. Kiszko was cleared on appeal after it became clear that forensic evidence, which was available to the police but which was suppressed at the time of his trial and never revealed to the defence team, clearly showed that Kiszko could not have been responsible for the murder. That forensic evidence later resulted in the conviction of another man, 30 years after the murder. Although one of the police officers and scientists on the case were served with summonses for suppressing evidence at Kiszko's trial, it was stayed by a magistrate on the grounds that the head of the inquiry had since died, and too much time had passed for a fair trial. It is a striking example of the unwritten code that allows self-censorship and miscarriages of justice to take place.

In contrast, the actions of Dr Stephen Bolsin led to major changes in the UK to paediatric cardiac surgery and to audit of surgical procedures, and across the world to reforms in clinical governance. These reforms have probably saved thousands of lives. The events in Bristol and the treatment of Dr Bolsin also led to the Public Interest Disclosure Act, which it was hoped would protect whistleblowers. Unfortunately the Act is flawed and has created additional problems for whistleblowers. Minor deviations from an institution's procedures, which are often complex, are commonly used to discipline or sack whistleblowers and hence deter others.

Dr Stephen Bolsin before giving evidence at the inquiry into the scandal over the high death rate of children undergoing cardiac surgery, 22 November 1999
Credit: Barry Batchelor/PA

Despite catalysing major improvements in medical care, Dr Bolsin found his position in Bristol untenable and he left. He was unable to get another post in the UK and he was forced to leave the country. Many other whistle-blowers have also suffered. Dr Rita Pal, who raised concerns about the care of elderly patients in Stoke-on-Trent, is no longer working as a doctor. Dr Kim Holt raised concerns about St Ann's child development clinic in Haringey run by Great Ormond Street Hospital. If her warnings had been heeded it might have prevented the death of Baby P. Instead she was suspended for four years before recently receiving an apology from the hospital. There are many other examples, but the message for anyone considering blowing the whistle is that you do so at your peril. Managers of institutions do not want to employ people who might expose bad practice and colleagues are afraid to work with them.

On one occasion when I reported dishonesty by a senior doctor, I was asked whether other doctors who knew of the misconduct were prepared to support my account of events. I asked five doctors who were witnesses and therefore able to corroborate my statement, but all refused to do so. None of them disputed my version of the events, but some said that exposure of such a senior doctor would harm the public's respect for the medical profession; others said that it would be bad for their careers and one said that what he had done was the sort of thing any doctor might do. (I would add that I would not.) My complaint did not progress, but several years later the senior doctor appeared in court because his dishonesty was repeated. We don't know whether in this case there were any other instances of dishonesty in the intervening period, but there is obviously a risk of harm to patients if wrongdoing by senior doctors is not supported and taken seriously by fellow doctors.

It is often difficult to determine how much self-censorship is out of loyalty to colleagues or institutions and how much is the fear of the retribution they might face if they blow the whistle. However, there is no doubt that the defamation laws, particularly in England and Wales, are a powerful incentive to self-censor.

I spent nearly four years fighting three defamation claims (for both libel and slander) brought in the English High Court by a US medical device corporation, NMT Medical. The cases started after I spoke at a cardiology conference in the USA about a clinical trial that was sponsored by NMT and in which I was the principal cardiologist. Some of my concerns about the research were published on a US website and they have subsequently been shown to have been justified. Others knew about the concerns, but they were not prepared to speak out either about that research or about the conduct of NMT. The legal cases ended recently when NMT went into liquidation. Only then did it become clear that some doctors had additional concerns about other devices made by NMT, but they had not reported them, even to official government regulators. Because it was clear that NMT was prepared to use the draconian English defamation laws to attack and silence critics of their devices, it had a chilling effect on the willingness of other doctors to report their concerns.

My experience of being sued for libel for raising legitimate concerns that affected public health echoed the experiences of Simon Singh, who was sued by the British Chiropractic Association; Dr Ben Goldacre, who was sued by Matthias Rath; and Dr Henrik Thomsen, who was sued by GE Healthcare. The publicity of these cases has had the unfortunate chilling effect of making others reluctant to speak out. We have no idea how many times people with justified concern about matters of public safety are deterred from reporting their concerns for fear of being sued for defamation.

If society wants people to speak out when there is a matter of public concern, we need to make it more culturally acceptable to speak out, to bring in laws that really do protect whistleblowers and to change the defamation laws so that they cannot be used by dishonest individuals and incompetent organisations to prevent exposure of matters of public concern. ❏

©Peter Wilmshurst
40(4): 149/154
DOI: 10.1177/0306422011429507
www.indexoncensorship.org

Peter Wilmshurst is consultant cardiologist, Royal Shrewsbury Hospital, and senior lecturer in medicine, University of Keele

FIRST PERSON

Writing from Algeria, Iran and
Western Sahara

Algiers, Algeria, 2000
Credit: Ted Pink/Alamy

A LESSON IN TYRANNY

Torture is a thing of the past in Algeria, says novelist **Boualem Sansal**. The authorities have a new doctrine for controlling the population

The place is charming. Luxury, peace and pleasure are the words that spring to mind as one walks down this peaceful street in the hills of Algiers. This shady peak affords a magnificent view of the bay of Algiers which Algerians claim is the most beautiful in the world. We feel proud to be from these shores, born in the cradle of civilisation that is the Mediterranean. What gods have presided here, what conquerors have passed this way, what wonders were conceived in these comings and goings, and what tragedies, too, vast and unforgettable.

The villa I want to talk about is located in this romantic setting, at the highest point of the popular neighbourhood of Belcourt where the *quartier* of Cervantès ends and Diar El Mahçoul begins, not far from the Stalinist Memorial of the Revolution which children in Algiers call *Houbel*, after a god from the pre-Islamic Arabic pantheon, protector of thieves and murderers.

Passing this magnificent Hispano-Moorish palace which recalls the finest moments of mythical Andalusia, one feels a longing to own it, to live the high life there, dreams which would require too much money, too many influential connections. The palace is a listed monument and the headquarters of a very useful public service. Not much is visible from the road — the high surrounding walls afford only a glimpse of the upper storey of the building, the stepped terraces, the frieze of decorative green tiles and tops of the many majestic trees. The grounds are lush and filled with multi-coloured flowers whose heady scents carry far on the breeze. The rest is easy to imagine. Algiers has more than its share of prestigious Hispano-Moorish villas. Not all are ringed with walls of stone – it is possible to admire the finely carved doors and windows, the spiral staircases, the verandas, the glinting mosaics, the covered walkways of pink gravel, the pools shimmering in the sunlight, the ancient trees, the banks of flowers. With a little luck, one might see young women in long gossamer dresses like princesses from the *Thousand and One Nights*, or even a genie in a *djelleba*, with a goatee beard, appearing from a lamp or through a wall. Perhaps he is the guardian of these beauties. Type 'Villa Sésini' into Google and this marvel will appear in all its white, mysterious splendour.

The palace does indeed bear this name: Villa Sésini. It was the French, when Algeria with its people and chattels belonged to them, who gave it this name and it has remained in our memories. This villa is famous the world over. Older Algerians shudder at the very name. So many of their families, their childhood friends, died in the cellars here in excruciating agony. During the Algerian War (1954–1962) the villa was a torture centre run by the legionnaires, the famous Leopards of the 1er REP (1st Foreign Parachute Regiment), who spearheaded the fight against the Algerian rebels. Here, dashing colonels like Aussaresse, Bigeard, Trinquier, not forgetting the young lieutenant Jean-Marie Le Pen – the future founder of the Front National and Holocaust denier before the Almighty – made their names.

There were dozens of torture centres around the city, hundreds scattered throughout the country. Many were bigger, better equipped, more terrifying, more efficient, run by this or that army unit or police division, but it is the Villa Sésini which has lived on in memory and in history books. It is a symbol of the torture carried out on a massive scale by a state, and not just any state – by the French state, by France, the birthplace of human rights. Undoubtedly its fame owes something to the villa's exceptional beauty, to the terrifying murderous reputation the legionnaires made for themselves in the *djebels*, to the efficacy of their interrogation techniques and the results obtained. It is because the French won the Battle of Algiers by these methods, by torturing the inhabitants of the city, sparing neither women nor children, that they lost the Algerian War. And it is because the Algerian rebels carried out terrorist attacks on civilians, including women and

Villa Sésini, the site of torture during the Algerian war (1954–1962)
Credit: Nicolas Tikhomiroff/Magnum Photos

children, that their victory has a bitter aftertaste of defeat. They lost all notion of freedom, which led to the harshest, most miserable dictatorship imaginable. As a man sins, so shall he be punished: that is the lesson of history. Fifty years later, the two countries are still arguing over their bad memories. Here we talk of torture, there they talk of terrorism, the twin faces of dishonour.

After independence, it was decided to turn the villa into a Museum of Torture exhibiting the various devices used by the French army: the famous *gégène* (a hand-cranked generator for charging field telephones, adapted as a torture device for electric shocks), the electric chair, the bath, the bar, the bottles, the whips, together with eyewitness accounts from those unfortunates who were interrogated here. Then the idea was abandoned, for fear that in a diplomatic tit-for-tat, a Museum of Terrorism would be built in Paris; besides, the air was thick with greed – high-ranking officials who coveted this magnificent palace and dreamed of getting their hands on it quietly contrived for it to remain vacant. After several years of covert struggle, the dignitaries gave up and the palace was assigned to a new government department.

Then history returned to normal and torture returned to the fore. The government of independent Algeria quickly discovered it had the noble soul of a torturer. It could not bear for the populace to dream of freedom or talk of hope. It adopted the methods of its former enemy, methods that had proved their worth during the Battle of Algiers: random arrests of as many people as possible – in the streets, at their work, from their homes, on the strength of anonymous tip-offs, vague evidence. Take men, women, children, separate them using torture and, afterwards, make the corpses disappear. Places of torture multiplied endlessly, repression was legalised and classified as revolutionary public-spiritedness in order to facilitate the work of civil servants and increase productivity. In this way it could be practised openly, at any time, in any place – in police stations, in army barracks, in the offices of the government and of the ruling party and, when discretion is required, in secret locations. If the victim is a foreigner, or someone famous, the work is delegated, subcontracted to unofficial police units, to underworld thugs, to Islamists from the mountains, to death squads, to jobless young men from the suburbs. The guiding principle of the government is simple: think big, so big it seems incredible since the incredible has the power to fire the imagination and therefore truly terrorise the populace, to paralyse it and drown the truth in a torrent of hysterical rumours.

Techniques have not progressed, as one might assume. On the contrary they have regressed, and in this lies their success: people are tortured as they were during the Holy Roman Inquisition, flesh is flayed, skin burned, bones broken, nails ripped out. The tools used are banal: salt, acid, fire, water, sticks, kitchen knives, pliers, gimlets, garrottes, vices, ropes, chains, nails, in fact whatever comes to hand, whatever springs to mind. The government did not think it worthwhile to train specialist torturers or to resort to modern technology, chemistry, psychology, brainwashing – all the clean, efficient techniques Naomi Klein straightforwardly discusses in her famous book *The Shock Doctrine*.

In recent years, there has been a real revolution. People no longer believe in the power of torture. It is something that belongs to the past, to the Cold War, a period that is over. The new doctrine might be summarised thus: why waste time torturing poor wretches to terrorise populations who, in any case, know nothing, when you can kill the populace itself. Duly noted. The game is on a massive scale: people are killed by category: by age, by profession, by region. They are tortured by starvation, unemployment, boredom, despair, isolation, humiliation, they are shut away in moral misery, they are driven to suicide, to throwing themselves into the sea, to immolating themselves, to killing each other, to disappearing forever – they, and their children. The final act: the survivors are driven to riot so they can be slaughtered by canon in the name of the legitimate upholding of public order. Afterwards, they are discredited in the eyes of international opinion – they are portrayed as murderers, subversives, terrorists, mercenaries.

It is an infallible method, perfected year upon year. The Americans did this superbly in Iraq. Abu Ghraib, Guantanamo, the secret prisons scattered all over the world, subcontractors working at every level, the whole world spied on, tapped – it beats everything. The Russians did not skimp in Chechnya, they turned that cheerful country into the Tartar Steppe. Arabic governments in turn have joined in, inspired by the Arab Spring: why bother to catch the fish when all you need to do is drain the sea? No life, no unrest, no trouble, the mud will suffocate them all. In 100 million years, they will be transformed into crude oil.

That is the conclusion of history.

Villas like the Villa Sésini, the dark, foul-smelling basements where suspects are abused, where the torturer exhausts himself interrogating some broken wretch, that is the past, it is history. Nowadays, whole peoples are wiped out, the sea is drained, the mountains levelled, the cities burned, memories erased, silence is imposed across the planet.

Times have changed. ❏

©Boualem Sansal
Translated by Frank Wynne
40(4): 157/161
DOI: 10.1177/0306422011427624
www.indexoncensorship.org

Boualem Sansal is the author of *An Unfinished Business* (Bloomsbury) and *Post Restante: Algiers, a letter of anger and hope to my compatriots*. His books are banned in his native Algeria. He was awarded the German Publishers and Booksellers Association Peace Prize in 2011

WET NIGHT OF DELIVERANCE

A short story by **Alireza Mahmoudi Iranmehr**

I felt like I wasn't done after I had cut off his head. Could it be this easy? He didn't have a name yet, but ever since I ran off with Reza seven years ago, I had always wanted to name my son Arash. I believe someone named Arash will never sleep with his own daughter, or set himself on fire with a gallon of gasoline.

Six days ago when he was born, it felt like I had found buried treasure. It was worth the pain of delivery. In the prison infirmary, when they told me it was a boy, it was as if my 5,300 tomans had won a black Mercedes in Tejarat Bank's raffle.

But then they said that they had to take Arash away. The judge had not allowed me to keep him. I didn't want them to take away my treasure. So what if my HIV positive blood is running through his veins? This is only stronger proof that he is mine. He doesn't belong to any of the thousands of people who meet you for a night, do their thing, and are gone forever. He is a piece of myself, outside, that I can hold in my arms and look at. It was the first time that someone had slept so peacefully next to me.

I stole the razor from inside Mrs Taghavi's prayer book. She secretly uses it for shaping the eyebrows of the other girls. This was the last night I would put my son to sleep next to me. When Bulky Shaheen's bed started creaking, I undid my blouse and nursed him. It had been years since I had felt so light-headed from a touch to my breasts. Then I held his mouth tight until he stopped breathing and began to cut off his head with the small razor. He didn't make a sound, and barely moved. The blade was dull and broken and kept cutting my fingers. I was thinking that a person couldn't die this easily; that he may still be alive even if his eyes are shut. I didn't want them to take away my treasure in such a completely perfect state, even if his eyes were shut. Maybe tomorrow he would open them in another room, would nurse at another woman's breasts, breathing just like he does as he suckles mine. I had kept my eyes shut the entire time when the nine of them were going at me all night long in that house north of Piroozi Square, but I hadn't died. All through that snowy February night, when I slept in a covered ditch at the intersection of College Avenue, I kept wondering about how a person dies. The rats ran through my hair. Their bodies were cold but they were alive and constantly moving all over me.

Bulky Shaheen's bed was seriously creaking now. I liked how the blood from my fingertips mixed with my son's. I had had a similar feeling as he was growing inside me. I sharpened the razor using a stone I had found in the prison yard. The rubbing of the blade over the stone sounded like the breathing of an innocent animal in the dark. It reminded me of the story of Abraham and how, to cut off his son's head, he had sharpened his knife on the mountain rocks, and yet the knife still wouldn't cut. But my razor blade, no bigger than a fingertip, cut really well.

I wanted to see the shape of his heart, a heart that was beating inside my own body until only six days ago. What does a person's life look like? I remembered the poems I used to read for Reza next to the Bosphorus. We were waiting to fill a book with them. In all my poems I used the word 'heart' over and over again. Removing Arash's heart with that tiny, slippery blade was difficult. Each time I pressed harder the blade kept cutting my own fingers. But when I finally removed it and held it in my hands, I saw that just like his birth, it had been worth the trouble. It was moist, small, and slippery, and shone in the dim light coming in from the corridor. It was as if he had been born a second time.

I held his heart in my hands and looked at it and wondered how can a person die? I had asked this question on many nights. The refrigerator seller at the corner of Amir Hozoor Street, who used to pay me 200,000 tomans to let him put out his cigarette in my belly button, used to say that one doesn't

Woman in Qom, Iran.
Credit: Omid Salehi
Omid Salehi: A Photographer's Journey through Iran *is*
published by Beyond Art Production, roseissa.com

die from these things. But Reza died very easily. They stabbed him with a knife in front of the bakery in Istanbul, he held his stomach, fell to the ground, and died. It was so quick that he didn't even have time to wonder about how one dies.

I squeezed my son's small, moist heart in my fist. Maybe this is where a person's life seeps out. Or maybe it is buried in a different place. One of the inmates was cursing in her sleep. I could smell the cigarette smoke from the students' cell all the way over here. I had taken my university exam books with me when I left for Turkey with Reza, but then I threw them all away. Later I wanted to find a book that explained how a person dies. I felt that I must search further inside his chest, like a book that you want to read to the very end.

He didn't even have time to wonder about how one dies

Forty-three nights after Reza died, as I was returning from Istanbul, I wished that I could find a part in my body that I could squeeze to end it all. That night, for the first time, I slept with the bus driver who bought me a sandwich and let me ride in the back of his bus all the way to Tehran. His breath smelled of cigarettes and sunflower seeds. His movements sometimes became one with the motion of the bus. But I just kept staring at the plastic heart that spun around hanging from the ceiling. I thought the heart kept getting larger and larger, and then smaller again. Near daybreak, when the driver returned to his seat, I pulled aside the velvet curtains. I stared at the sky through the red stickers that spelled out something on the rear window. The last stars were disappearing in the light of dawn.

A dim white light was shining into the cell from the small opening near the ceiling. I couldn't tell if it was daybreak or if someone had lit the gas lamp in the prison yard. Someone was snoring in her sleep.

Bulky Shaheen was finally silent. A faint singing could be heard from a distance. My fingers were burning. My hands were wet all the way to my wrists. I had lost the blade among the small pieces left of my son. But now, no one would be taking him away. No one could hurt him. I had no more dreams left. After running away with Reza, this was the first thing I had done for myself. This wet night of deliverance was worth the burning feeling in my hands, and the loss of a small razor blade. ❐

This story is dedicated to Soraya. It was inspired by the sensational trial of a woman called Soheila in Iran. She was accused of killing and dismembering her five-day-old baby, who had Aids. She said that she killed the baby because she did not want the infant to suffer the same bitter fate as her. She was also accused of working as a prostitute. During the trial, she said repeatedly that she had worked as a prostitute because she had no choice and in order to earn a living.

© Alireza Mahmoudi Iranmehr
Translated by Sanam Kalantari
40(4): 163/167
DOI: 10.1177/0306422011427626
www.indexoncensorship.org

Alireza Mahmoudi Iranmehr is an Iranian short story writer, screenplay writer, critic and lecturer on modern literary fiction. He has published two short story collections, *Berim Khoshgozaruni* (Let's Go Have a Ball, 2005) and *Abr-e Surati* (Pink Cloud, 2008). The first collection is currently banned

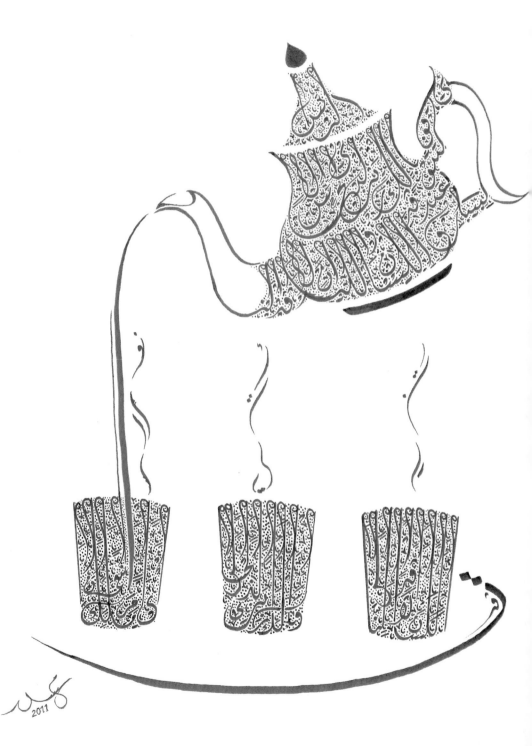

HOW TO MAKE TEA

Mustapha Abdel Dayem's short story gives a revealing glimpse of the Saharawi people's daily life, culture and aspirations

'I do not understand how the world can continue watching these barbaric scenes without reacting,' says Mustapha Abdel Dayem, recalling the Moroccan authorities' brutal attacks on Saharawi protesters in late 2010. A writer and journalist born in Morocco in 1962, he has been championing the plight of the people of Western Sahara for over two decades.

Western Sahara, located along the Atlantic coast between Morocco and Mauritania, has been the subject of a dispute between Morocco and the Polisaro Front, the Saharawi liberation movement fighting for independence. When Spain ended its colonial rule in 1975, the territory was jointly invaded by Morocco and Mauritania, provoking a 16-year war, ending in a UN-brokered ceasefire in 1991. Meanwhile, Morocco had completed the building of a defensive 'berm' in 1987, a sand wall stretching 2,200 kilometres dividing the length of Western Sahara and enclosing four-fifths of the territory under its occupation. All initiatives since the 1991 ceasefire to bring about a peaceful solution in the region have ended in deadlock.

Most Saharawi people now live in refugee camps – the estimated number of displaced people living in camps ranges from 100,000 to 170,000 – run by

the Polisario Front in south-western Algeria in one of the harshest desert environments in the world. A significant Saharawi population also live in Western Sahara under Moroccan occupation but as second-class citizens in their own homeland, with virtually no rights or freedoms. So while conditions are poor in the refugee camps, it is a space that at least affords the Saharawis some measure of freedom, dignity and representation. Healthcare, schools and the government in exile all operate from within the camps, supporting the refugee population there, though food shortages are an ongoing problem and those wanting and able to pursue education beyond primary school level must travel outside the territory. The Saharawi boast a strong civil society network within the territory – Sahara Press Service, Western Sahara TV and saharatoday.net are among the media outlets available to and serving the communities.

It is against this background that Mustapha Abdel writes, combining a raw realism with lyrical snapshots of a disenfranchised people, culture and history, drawing on the region's literary allegorical tradition. His early writing was published in Moroccan newspapers, but following the 2005 uprising in Western Sahara, his work took on a more political edge, reporting on human rights violations perpetrated by the authorities – though it did not touch specifically on the campaign for independence. 'A Lesson on How to Make Tea', published below, was written in 2008, just months before Abdel Dayem was imprisoned on 27 October for allegedly desecrating the Moroccan flag, destruction of public property and inciting armed unrest. Since then, the Moroccan authorities have been wary of him, seeing his writing as controversial and a potential threat to their control in the territory. Held in Tiznit prison near Rabat in overcrowded conditions, he was denied medical treatment and told that he would not be able to engage in educational activities after his release. 'Writing is a dangerous risk,' he admitted in a telephone interview from his prison cell in early 2011. In July 2011, Abdel Dayem was taken from his cell along with another Saharawi writer. For several days, his family and supporters did not know of his whereabouts.

Abdel Dayem continued to write while in prison, documenting the Saharawis' political aspirations, describing prison conditions, revealing the profound mental and physical pain of hunger strikes, extreme isolation and the pervasive silence around the ongoing plight. In early 2010, the Union of Saharawi Writers and Journalists and the Saharawi Ministry of Culture published Ureed Fajran! (I Want a Dawn!), a collection of Abdel Dayem's writing published in Arabic. The collection was shortlisted for the Freedom to Create prize category for imprisoned artists.

Mustapha Abdel Dayem was released on 27 October 2011.

A Saharawi man stands near the goat pens at a refugee camp, el Aauin, Algeria
Credit: Andrew McConnell/Panos

He leant on his left side as he began tipping the tea into the cups with his right hand. Underneath the *tabla*, a round tray on small legs, was a copy of the novel *The Mother* by the famous Russian writer Maxim Gorky. He would go back to reading this whenever he put the kettle over the weak coal fire. The water boiled slowly and the dry tea leaves opened up, revealing whatever dirt had stuck onto them. Before lifting the kettle from the coal, he put a rial note between the pages of the novel and then closed it. He held the kettle gently and poured out the blood-red liquid. The tea leaves had gathered at the bottom. He added a little water and stirred the kettle lightly, then emptied the contents in one scoop to free them of any residue.

He opened the novel at the page where he had put the rial. It was perhaps the only piece of Moroccan currency that did not carry the face of the king, maybe because of its value, just five centimes. The hungry stomachs are searching for a bite to eat anywhere and at any price, even under the earth. The miners are going into the depths of the earth to extract the rich minerals, but they might not get out. The mother alone awaits their return. Some drops of tea slid out from the kettle and fell onto the coal. The smoke and the smell of tea made him hurriedly put the rial between the pages of the novel once again. He filled the glass with red-coloured tea. The froth rose as the liquid was poured out, quickly yet carefully, into the small glass. He put what sugar there was into the kettle, wanting the tea to be the desired trio: hot, sweet and thick.

There is a huge difference between those who own the mines and those who work in them. The mother hopes to see her sons in good health and to find what she will provide for them, the fair distribution of resources.

He offered cups of tea to the groups of people on his right, moving from them to those on his far left, pouring each of them an equal amount of the liquid. Everyone drank from their cups in quick gulps, feeling it flowing through their veins, reviving the vitality of their bodies and taking away the worries from their minds.

Everyone drank from their cups in quick gulps

'*Bi-sihhat il-qayyam.*' To the health of the tea maker. They repeated this, one after the other, praising the quality of the tea as they returned the empty cups. He wanted to arrange them on the *tabla* again before returning to the page where he had put the Moroccan rial to mark where he had stopped reading his novel. He wiped the sweat from his forehead with his palm and looked at the teapot over the coal. He knew that this was 'the middle cup', the most important in the three Saharawi cycles of drinking tea. It was not important if the first cup was 'thick' or if the third was sweet. What mattered was that the second cup should satisfy everyone's tastes. For the Saharawis, it was acceptable to forgo the first and last cups of tea but they always wanted to taste the middle cup.

He nodded his head as he wondered what remained of Maxim Gorky and his novel *The Mother*. He had predicted the revolution but not her fate. He noticed the tea was boiling in the teapot and being pushed to the top. He quickly lifted the teapot and poured the tea into the cups packed together on the *tabla*.

His eyes roamed over the group around him reading quietly, engrossed in Hussein Marwah, Jean-Jacques Rousseau, John Dewey, Dostoyevsky, Nizar Qabbani and others, and listening to the music of Mariem Mint el Hassan. He smiled to himself and turned towards the pile of books, taking the first one he came across. Its title was *War and Peace*. He quickly flipped through its pages and was delighted to find the ribbon fixed inside as a bookmark. He returned to his seat and began to tip the tea into the cups while thinking about how to get rid of the Moroccan rial, which he no longer needed now he had this ribbon fixed inside the novel *War and Peace*. ❐

For more information about Western Sahara and free expression, visit sandblast-arts.org

©Mustapha Abdel Dayem
Translated by Razia Ali
40(4): 169/173
DOI: 10.1177/0306422011427621
www.indexoncensorship.org

A censorship chronicle incorporating science stories from the *Age*, al Jazeera, AsiaOne, BBC, CNN, *Guardian*, Huffington Post, Network for Education and Academic Rights (NEAR), *Nature*, *New Scientist*, *New York Times* (*NYT*), Sense About Science, *Telegraph* and organisations affiliated with the International Freedom of Expression Exchange (IFEX)

Australia

In June 2011, a weight-loss product manufacturer, SensaSlim, announced plans to sue a critic for libel, despite the fact that its assets had already been frozen by a consumer watchdog. Melbourne academic **Dr Ken Harvey** had complained to the Complaints Resolution Panel and the Therapeutic Goods Administration (a government regulatory body) about the way SensaSlim was being promoted. In response, SensaSlim launched a defamation action claiming damages for libel for the sum of A$800,000 (US$750,000) plus costs. In the same month, the Australian Competition and Consumer Commission won an order freezing SensaSlim's assets, as it emerged that research used to market the company's products had been fabricated. (the *Age*, the *Conversation*, Sense About Science)

Editor-in-chief of the *Australian*, Chris Mitchell, threatened to sue **a former reporter** for defamation in November 2010 because she allegedly claimed reporting about climate change at the paper was 'absolutely excruciating'. (theaustralian.com)

Azerbaijan

Rafig Aliyev was dismissed as chairman of the Department of the Automated Management Systems of the State Oil Academy on 7 November 2011. The move followed his participation in the Forum of Azerbaijani Intelligentsia on 4 November, which called for intellectuals to speak out against injustice in the country. (Azerireport)

Bahrain

A **group of medics** went on hunger strike in September 2011 to protest against their trial in a military court. The medics were arrested for treating wounded protesters during a crackdown on pro-democracy demonstrations earlier in the year. According to a former chairman of the Shia al Wefaq organisation, civilians should not be tried in a military court because it is against the country's constitution. (al Jazeera, European Phoenix)

Belgium

The vice president of the UN Intergovernmental Panel on Climate Change attempted to ban a lecture by climate change sceptic **Dr S Fred Singer** in August 2011. Jean-Pascal van Ypersele questioned Singer's 'scientific integrity' ahead of his scheduled speech at SEII Fondation Universitaire in Brussels and wrote to the university, stating that any links between Singer or his ideas and the university would be 'scandalous'. The venue for the event was changed and Singer's speech went ahead. (*American Thinker*)

Canada

In August 2011, federal fisheries scientist **Kristi Miller** was barred from talking to the press regarding her environmental research. Miller discovered a virus which may have been killing salmon in the Fraser River before they reached their spawning grounds. The research was published in *Science*, but the researcher was told by Ottawa's Privy Council Office not to speak to the press to avoid 'influencing' the ongoing federal inquiry into the decline of the Fraser sockeye salmon. The Privy Council Office's decision was later withdrawn. (Huffington Post)

Scientists working for Natural Resources Canada, a government ministry, were prevented from releasing their findings in October 2010. The employees were informed that they must get permission first, with the implication that they may be prevented from releasing unfavourable data. The scientists created the blog PublicScience.ca, which aims to 'speak up for science' by bringing government scientists face to face with Canadians and openly discussing their research findings. (Ubyssey)

China

Hundreds of protesters gathered at a solar panel factory in Haining, Zhejiang province, on 18 September 2011 after local residents complained that the factory was polluting the surrounding area, resulting in health problems among the population. Around 500 people burst into the compound of Jinko Solar Holding Company, demanding that the factory be relocated. (*Guardian*)

A journalist investigating a food scandal was stabbed to death in Henan in September 2011. **Li Xiang**, from Luoyang Television Station, had been reporting on the sale of cooking oil made from food waste found in gutters. He was stabbed more than 10 times and his laptop was stolen. Xiang's investigations led to the arrests of 32 people, who were caught selling the carcinogenic product. (AsiaOne)

In August 2011, some 2000 people were arrested and nearly 5000 businesses shut down as authorities attempted to raise **food safety standards** by clamping down on illegal food additives. The country has suffered a spate of scandals in the food industry. In April 2011, three children died and a further 35 were hospitalised after drinking milk contaminated with nitrite. In 2008, at least six babies died and up to 300,000 people fell sick after consuming milk powder laced with melamine. (BBC, *New Scientist*)

Denmark

A leading Danish radiologist claimed in December 2009 that UK libel laws had prevented him from talking about his research. **Henrik Thomsen** refused to talk about findings from his work in England out of fear of being sued for libel. His decision followed a case against him from a subsidiary of General Electric, which claimed he defamed it at a conference in 2007 when he said a drug manufactured by GE Healthcare had potentially fatal side effects. The company dropped the libel action in February 2010. Thomsen said he feared the health of patients in England is at risk because the scientific community is prevented from sharing its knowledge. (*Guardian*)

International

A number of organisations called on the United Nations to champion **access to information laws**, transparency and free media as key requirements to environmental and human sustainability in November 2011. The submission by 77 organisations also called for a new international convention governing access to justice in environmental matters and a UN Freedom of Information Act. (ARTICLE 19, *Colombo Telegraph*)

Iran

Nuclear scientist **Dariaush Rezaie** was shot and killed in July 2011, the latest in a string of attacks against nuclear researchers in the country. **Majid Shahriari** of the Shahid Beheshti University in Tehran was killed and nuclear physicist **Dr Fereidoun Abbasi** was injured in separate attacks on 29 November 2010 and physicist **Masoud Ali Mohammadi** was killed by a bomb attack on 12 January 2010. In January 2011, there were reports that **Shahram Amiri** had not been seen since his return to the country following his allegations that he had been abducted and tortured by the CIA. Observers outside Iran claimed that Amiri had returned from the US because there were threats against his family and that he was imprisoned and tortured by Iranian authorities after being accused of giving away state secrets. Iran's nuclear agency blamed Israeli agents and the US for the murders of and attacks on the scientists, accusing them of trying to disrupt Iran's nuclear programme. (BBC, MSNBC, *NYT*, *Telegraph*)

An Iranian physics student was accused of spying in early 2011. **Omid Kokabee**, an Iranian graduate student at the University of Texas in Austin, was due to go on trial in August 2011 after being accused of 'communicating with a hostile government' and 'illegal earnings', but the trial was postponed. Kokabee, who was imprisoned in February 2011, was arrested by the Iranian security services while trying to leave Iran. Kokabee's trial began on 4 October. (Huffington Post, *Nature*)

Iraq

In 2011, insurgents killed several academics, researchers and scientists, among them **Zaid Abdul Munim**, head of research at the molecular department at Mustansiriya University, on 3 April; **Mohammed Alwan**, dean of the faculty of medicine at al Mustansiriya University and prominent surgeon, killed on 29 March; Professor **Saad Abduljabbar** of the Technological University in Baghdad, killed on 27 February; and **Ali Shalash**, professor of poultry diseases at the College of Veterinary Medicine in Baghdad, killed on 17 February. (NEAR)

Italy

On 25 May 2011, it was announced that **six Italian seismologists and a government official** will face trial for manslaughter after the advice they gave prior to the 2009 earthquake in L'Aquila was deemed inadequate by an Italian court. The seismologists took part in a meeting of Italy's Major Risks Committee to assess evidence from early warning tremors. They found no reason to indicate that these tremors were likely to lead to a large quake. A major earthquake registering 6.3 on the Richter scale hit the L'Aquila area on 6 April 2009, killing 309 people. The prospect of the trial raised concerns among the scientific community, with several experts responding that earthquakes cannot be predicted with sufficient skill and accuracy to justify a full evacuation in advance. (Sense About Science)

Japan

A **heavily redacted document** detailing the 11 March 2011 accidents at the Fukushima plant in Tokyo was submitted to a special science committee in August 2011. Tokyo Electric Power Co (Tepco) submitted two manuals for accidents and severe accidents to assist with establishing the cause of the disaster, but it was reported that the six-page document on nuclear accidents was almost unreadable because it had been so severely marked up. Tepco resubmitted the manuals on 9 September. (*Mainichi Daily News*)

Mexico

The body of a genome specialist was found dismembered in August 2011. **Yadira Dávila Martínez**, who worked for the Universidad Nacional Autónoma de México, the country's top public university, disappeared from a shopping centre in Cuernavaca on 5 August. Her body was discovered just over a week later in the town of Temixco. The discovery followed the attack on nanotechnology professor **Armando Herrera Corral and a colleague**, who were injured by a bomb sent by an anti-technology group to Tecnológico de Monterrey on 8 August. (CNN Mexico, *El Universal*)

Peru

A scientist had his conviction for character defamation overturned in December 2010. **Dr Ernesto Bustamante** faced a prison sentence for speaking to the media and writing a newspaper article disagreeing with another molecular biologist who had claimed local maize varieties were contaminated with transgenes. Before the conviction was overturned, Bustamante was forbidden from leaving Lima without a judge's permission and was forced to present himself on the last day of every month to the court to sign a register. Bustamante also paid US$1,800 damages to the defendant. (*Nature*, Sense About Science)

Russia

Dr Igor Sutyagin, a nuclear scientist and former head of division at the Russian Academy of Sciences in Moscow, was released from prison on 9 July 2010. Sutyagin had been detained by the Russian Federal Security Service (FSB) in October 1999, charged with espionage and sentenced to 15 years' imprisonment. He was accused of passing classified information to a research firm in London. Sutyagin had been conducting freelance analysis of civilian-military relations in Russia at the time of his arrest. He claimed that, as a civilian researcher, he had no access to classified sources. Sutyagin was released along with 11 individuals alleged by the US government to be Russian spies. (NEAR)

Somalia

Twenty-two young **medics, doctors and government ministers** were killed in a suicide bomb attack at a graduation ceremony in December 2009. The attack, at the Shamo Hotel in Mogadishu, injured 90 people. The graduates were only the second group of medical students to receive their diplomas in almost 20 years. The university was set up in 2002 to train doctors after many had fled the country or been killed in the civil war. (NEAR)

Turkey

Dr Çiğdem Atakuman, editor of the popular science magazine *Bilim ve Teknik* (Science and Technology), was dismissed in March 2009 after he planned to publish a 'controversial' cover story. The story, which celebrated the 200th anniversary of Charles Darwin's birth, was replaced by a feature on global warming. The cancellation of the feature was the latest in a series of conflicts between scientists and Islamic creationists in Turkey, many of them initiated by Adnan Oktar, who argues that evolution discredits Islam. Scientists also claim that the creationist organisation BAV has intimidated those who speak out against creationism. (Hurriyet, *New Scientist*)

Turkmenistan

Biologist and environmental activist **Andrei Zakota** was released from prison on 6 November 2009 after his five-year sentence was commuted and replaced by a fine of 1000 manat (US$350). It was widely believed that Zakota's imprisonment was a politically motivated move to silence the scientist. He was attacked without warning on 20 October 2009 and was arrested by two police officers at the scene. (NEAR)

United Kingdom

Government ministers were accused of refusing to fund vital research relating to the lethal brain disease CJD on 19 September 2011. Expert advisers said they believed that up to 15,000 people in the UK could carry the prion infection agents that cause variant Creutzfeldt-Jakob disease (vCJD), but that this figure was said to have been ignored or sidelined. Researchers argued that acknowledging the true figure would mean they could create precautionary measures that fit the scale of the problem. (*Guardian*)

Tobacco company Philip Morris International (PMI) used Scottish freedom of information laws to access research held by **Stirling University** regarding young people and smoking in September 2011. The university's Centre for Tobacco Control Research fought the move but was ordered to provide the required information. The research details attitudes to smoking and packaging. The director of the centre, Professor Gerard Hastings, said the tobacco company was mining his research for confidential data on children's attitudes to cigarettes. (BBC)

An Oxford academic won the right to read previously secret data on climate change in July 2011. **Jonathan Jones**, a physics professor at Oxford University, submitted a freedom of information request for the findings of research carried out by the head of the University of East Anglia's Climatic Research Unit, Phil Jones, in 2009. The unit initially refused to provide the data, but was forced to following a ruling by the information commissioner. The decision was hailed as a landmark ruling that will mean that thousands of British researchers will be required to share their data with the public. (*Guardian*)

British Medical Association (BMA) members voted in June 2011 to adopt into policy a call for a **stronger public interest defence** and a restriction on the ability of commercial organisations to sue for libel. (Sense About Science)

The British Chiropractic Association (BCA) dropped its defamation case against science writer **Simon Singh** on 15 April 2010. The BCA lodged a case against Singh after the publication of an article in the *Guardian* in which he criticised the association for defending chiropractors who treat conditions such as colic and asthma in children without having significant evidence that the treatment will be effective on the condition. The case, in which Singh received substantial support, was initially lodged by the BCA in 2008. (*Guardian*)

United States

In October 2011, a Texan oceanographer claimed his work was being censored after he submitted research to the state's environmental agency. **John Anderson** claimed that his report on the Galveston Bay estuary was altered prior to publication and that key information on the impact of climate change on the area had been omitted. Anderson believed that the state of Texas did not want to publish findings suggesting human contribution to global warming. *(Houston Chronicle)*

A study funded by the National Institutes of Health (NIH) found that **black scientists** with a PhD received 10 per cent fewer funding awards than white scientists or scientists from other ethnic minorities. The study, published on 19 August 2011, analysed over 80,000 applications for funding from scientists with a PhD. Of those, 1149 came from black applicants. Whites had a 29 per cent success rate for applications, while blacks received funding just 16 per cent of the time. When the researchers adjusted for country of origin, additional training, previous research awards, and publication record, the discrepancy was still 10 per cent. (*New Scientist*, sciencemag.org)

US government funding for **stem cell research** was blocked in late August 2010, following a judgment that ruled the research violates laws prohibiting the destruction of human embryos. The temporary injunction bars federal funding for studies on stem cells derived from human embryos that are later discarded. (*Guardian*)

Scientists investigating the deaths of dolphins in the area affected by the BP oil spill in the Gulf of Mexico in April 2010 were ordered by the government not to release their findings. Wildlife biologists working for the **National Marine Fisheries Service** were investigating the rise in dolphin mortality, but were told to keep their findings confidential as the cause of the deaths would form part of the ongoing federal criminal investigation into the disaster. (*Daily Mail*)

Compiled by Marta Cooper and Alice Purkiss
DOI: 10.1177/0306422011427796